Being an Effective Headteacher

Trevor Male

P·C·P

Paul Chapman
Publishing

Paul Chapman Publishing
A SAGE Publications Company
1 Oliver's Yard
55 City Road
London EC1Y 1SP

SAGE Publications Inc
2455 Teller Road
Thousand Oaks, California 91320

SAGE Publications India Pvt Ltd
B-42, Panchsheel Enclave
Post Box 4109
New Delhi 110 017

Library of Congress Control Number: 2006901999

A catalogue record for this book is available from the British Library

ISBN 10 1-4129-1997-5   ISBN 13 978-1-4129-1997-5
ISBN 10 1-4129-1998-3   ISBN 13 978-1-4129-1998-2 (pbk)

Typeset by Dorwyn Ltd, Wells, Somerset
Printed in Great Britain by Athenaeum Press, Gateshead, Tyne & Wear
Printed on paper from sustainable resources

To my son, Oliver. May he always enjoy effective headteachers.

Trevor Male

Trevor is a Senior Lecturer within the Centre for Educational Studies at the University of Hull where he is Director for the masters and doctoral programmes in educational leadership. He leads the university's provision for headteacher development and has worked as a trainer, assessor and consultant on National College for School Leadership (NCSL) programmes. Earlier in his career he served for eleven years as a teacher, for eight years as an LEA officer and was also a tutor/counsellor for the Open University for several years.

Trevor was awarded a PhD in Educational Leadership by the University of Lincoln in 2004 for his thesis on the personal, organizational and occupational dimensions of the transition to headship experienced by headteachers. His research interests are in the nature of school leadership and in the role of the headteacher in particular, where he has an extensive track record of research, publications and consultancy.

His work has been published widely in books and journals within the UK, the USA and elsewhere and he is a regular contributor to national and international conferences. He has established an excellent reputation both as a consultant and presenter on in-service activities both on a regional and national basis. In recent years he has been a Visiting Lecturer in the USA where he has strong links with colleagues from the universities of Northern Colorado, San Diego and Texas.

Contents

Glossary

CPD	Continuing Professional Development
DfES	Department for Education and Skills
EI	Emotional Intelligence
EQ	Emotional Quotient
GTC	General Teaching Council
HE	Higher Education
HEI	Higher Education Institution
HEADLAMP	Headteacher Leadership and Management Programme
HIP	Headteacher Induction Programme
HMI	Her Majesty's Inspectorate
INSET	In-service Education of Teachers
IPH	International Placement for Headteachers
ISLLC	Interstate School Leaders Licensure Consortium
ITE	Initial Teacher Education
LEA	Local Education Authority
LftM	Leading from the Middle
LPSH	Leadership Programme for Serving Headteachers
NAHT	National Association of Headteachers
NASSP	National Association of Secondary School Principals
NCSL	National College for School Leadership
NEAC	National Education Assessment Centre
NLE	National Leader of Education
NPQH	National Professional Qualification for Headship
OTTO	One Term Training Opportunities
PIL	Partnerships In Leadership
SHA	Secondary Headeachers Association
SMTF	School Management Task Force
TDA	Training and Development Agency
TTA	Teacher Training Agency
USP	Unique Selling Point

Introduction

This book is primarily based on the model of headship in England whereby each school has it own, unique, identity and serves a community which is usually geographically defined. The role of headteacher has evolved since the inception of a compulsory education system for the nation's children in the latter stages of the nineteenth century and is posited on the notion that not only should there be a formal head of the school but also that that person should be both responsible for and directly involved in the teaching and student learning taking place within.

The unique nature of headship in England does not mean, however, that the book is not relevant to those who operate in other school systems, as the theory bases explored in demonstrating the nature of headship will be significant to those responsible for developing school leaders at a local, national or international level and to scholars in the field of school leadership. As formal leaders of the school, headteachers and principals are central to organized education systems and are commonly seen as the most influential figure in the success of their student body. Coming to terms with the demands of the job really involves reconciling a range of personal values and beliefs with the demands of the system and feeling comfortable in that position. This is a reciprocal process with both the individual and the system exerting influence on each other. Comfort is achieved when the personal value system of the headteacher correlates closely with the actual and perceived demands of the school and the society it serves. Effective headteachers, therefore, meet the learning needs of the student body and do so within a moral code that is acceptable to all stakeholders within the school community to which they are appointed.

Headship in England is established within a matrix of governance and management systems that tend to distinguish the job from other, similar, positions held in other school systems. Whilst the regulations relating to maintained schools and the position of headteacher are shared with Wales, there are fundamental cultural differences that separate the two countries in terms of headship. Meanwhile structural differences and local political factors determine the task of formal school leadership in England generally to be different elsewhere in the United Kingdom and the rest of the world, with the exception of the nation's independent schools which tend to conform to similar social mores as those observed in the maintained sector.

There is an English factor which influences the model of headship explored here, therefore, with the consequence that the book is of direct relevance to anyone aspiring to headship and to newly appointed head-teachers in England, particularly those who are in the early stages of the transition to their new role. The contents will also be of interest to serving headteachers, however, who are seeking to achieve new understandings of their position and to re-shape their practice.

To complicate matters, this book is published at a juncture in the history of headship which may bring about significant changes to the nature of the job. At the time of writing there are significant problems with recruitment and retention nationally to this key school leadership post and to similar positions internationally. In England over 1500 headteacher jobs remained vacant at the beginning of 2006, with around 10 per cent of the nation's schools advertising for a new headteacher annually and re-advertisements reaching record levels. Conventional wisdom suggests that the challenges of the job have proved to be such that the post is no longer an attractive proposition for prospective headteachers. There is the distinct possibility that the traditional model of one headteacher for every school, which has been prevalent for most of the last century, is now compromised in the first instance by an absence of suitable candidates.

The demands on headteachers are also increasing with emphasis being placed on schools in England to widen their remit through the five point policy of 'Every Child Matters', which represents a more socially focused approach to child development than the more traditional academic expec-tations. The aim of central government is for every child, whatever their background or their circumstances, to have the support they need to be healthy, stay safe, enjoy and achieve, to make a positive contribution and achieve economic well-being. Consequently we have seen schools begin to offer a wider range of services and extend their provision. We can expect those demands to continue growing as the policy is underpinned by notions of multi-agency work being channelled through schools.

The twin factors of headteacher shortage and widening remit have led to a widespread expectation that the future success of the school system will be established through federating schools and developing system leader-ship as mechanisms for enhancing the quality of education. That discourse has reached policy levels, with the Secretary of State for Education indicat-ing in her remit letter to the National College for School Leadership (NCSL) in December, 2005, that one the college's priorities for the next two years was to develop a register of potential executive headteachers, whose leadership skills could be used to enhance the wider school system and to investigate ways in which to accredit them as National Leaders of Education (NLEs). The possible ramifications of such a move could mean that either we will see a radical transformation of school systems or of school leadership. A government-sponsored encouragement to federate schools, run by executive headteachers, could answer a number of endemic issues within the maintained sector, including a reduction in the number of surplus school places in the nation (estimated to be a million) and a concomitant reduction in the number of headteachers required. The deployment of NLEs to become an effective source of advice and guidance to schools nationally would thus supplement their emerging local role as executive headteachers, appointed to take charge of multiple school sites.

Those prospects are still in the early stages of evolution, however, and could well remain as either fanciful imaginings or manifest themselves in other ways. Certainly a high degree of political activity is evident at the national level in this debate and the ambitions for 'system leadership' may yet founder on the rock of educational conservatism. At this stage, therefore, it is unlikely that the demands on the majority of serving or prospective headteachers will be radically altered during the next five years. The headteacher will remain the key professional figure capable of effecting change and improvement for their designated school. Consequently this book is about preparing for and entering headship, focusing on the quest to become effective in that job at the earliest opportunity.

The evidence for my conclusions is drawn from a variety of sources including a wide experience of instrumental working relationships with national, local and institutional leadership development activities, assimilation in the theoretical basis of effective school leadership and an extensive record of empirical research in the field, nationally and internationally. I have been closely associated with most initiatives in leadership and management development for headteachers since the mid-1980s, having served as an LEA officer responsible for professional development, as a liaison officer to a central government task force for school management, as an accredited trainer and assessor for the National Professional Qualification for Headship (NPQH) and as a provider on the nationally funded entry to headship programmes of the Headteacher Leadership and Management Programme (HEADLAMP) and Headteacher Induction Programme (HIP). Throughout this time I have accumulated a wealth of unpublished documentary evidence through engagement with the development of these initiatives.

Meanwhile, in my day job, I have been responsible for devising and running programmes in educational leadership and management at doctoral and masters levels in three universities in the UK, have been accorded Visiting Lecturer status in several overseas universities, and have also run many non-accredited programmes for hundreds of aspirant and serving headteachers, each of whom has provided me with fresh insights into the most challenging leadership position in the school system. My specialist research interest is in the field of formal school leadership, particularly headteachers and other similar positions world wide, and I have accumulated a wealth of data from surveys and field-based investigations. A range of publications has appeared in academic and professional journals as a result of this research record and I have been a regular contributor to national and international research conferences on headteacher and principal development. I would claim, therefore, a knowledge of school leadership in action that allows me to make recommendations as to how to become effective in such posts.

Nationally and internationally there have been moves in the last decade of the twentieth century to ensure the quality of formal school leaders through the provision of licensure schemes, underwritten by standards derived from the examination of successful leadership practice in a variety of occupations. Although there is evidence to suggest that the quality of school leadership has improved overall, my investigations into the transition to formal school leadership would suggest that beginning headteachers and principals are not fully prepared for their new job (Male, 1996; Daresh and Male, 2000; Male and Merchant, 2000), with these findings being reflected in similar, contemporary studies (for example, Dunning, 1996; Draper and McMichael, 1998). For first-time headteachers the consensus was that only about one in six felt they were adequately prepared for the challenges of headship (Earley et al., 2003).

My analysis of those findings and other relevant literature leads me to conclude that the transition to successful formal leadership encompasses development along three dimensions before the newly appointed leader really feels able to exhibit mastery of the associated tasks and to be the major influence in terms of organizational function. I have classified the three dimensions as *personal, organizational* and *occupational* and would argue that the emphasis within licensure schemes has been on developing the occupational dimension, leaving the other two dimensions to form part of a process of natural adaptation by the incumbent.

This 'sink or swim' approach to leadership development is clearly inadequate in school systems that require the new leader to be effective almost immediately. Typically we can see newly appointed school leaders going through several stages of development before feeling competent and confident in their new role, with the prospect of that process lasting several years without adequate learning experiences before appointment and the provision of appropriate support mechanisms through the transition period. This book aims to explore the learning needs and challenges presented along each of the three dimensions in order to help reach that position more quickly. This general approach is then applied to the specific nature of headship in maintained and independent schools in England, seeking to aid individuals in their quest to become an effective headteacher.

At this stage I have chosen not to explore differences in headteacher style and behaviour that have been influenced by the gender, ethnicity or religion of the incumbent, preferring instead to focus on the nature of a job which still seeks common definition. As a nation we do not have a commonly accepted theory of headship and have tended to draw on theory and practice from other occupations or systems when identifying development opportunities. I believe we need such a theory in place before seeking to differentiate further. In time we could then establish dimensions of headship that are not only relevant to gender, ethnicity and religion, but also to the type, phase and context of individual schools. Those are tasks not to be taken lightly and ones that will not be undertaken in this edition of my work. Instead I have employed an asexual, amorphous model of headship with the intention that each reader will undertake the task of applying my conclusions to their circumstance.

The book is organized into seven chapters that focus on a career transition to that point where you feel comfortable, confident and competent in your new job, whether this is your first, second or multiple headship position. Chapters 1 and 2 establish the context and theory that underpin headship, with the remaining chapters charting the course to effective headship.

This book seeks to guide you through to effectiveness and is organized accordingly. Firstly we will explore the transition to formal leadership, in this case to the point where a headteacher feels competent and confident in role. To achieve that state, where you feel you have consolidated yourself within the job and the school, you will have explored: relevant literature and theory associated with the transition (Chapter 2); how to prepare for headship (Chapter 3); the content and value of the national standards for headteachers (Chapter 4); and how best to set about applying for and entering headship (Chapters 5 and 6). The final chapter aims to help you in your quest to reach the highest level, to become an effective headteacher. Chapter 7 will thus explore the consolidation and extension of headship whilst remembering that the first six chapters are essential to that level in much the same way that sound foundations are important to a good building and proper preparation leads to a better finish when decorating the house.

I still continue to investigate headship in the search for establishing effective theories for action and I would be delighted to hear from you if you think you could help me with this continuing research agenda. You can reach me by email at t.d.male@hull.ac.uk. I look forward to hearing your responses.

Acknowledgements

The author and publisher would like to thank the following for giving permission to use the following:

Figures 3.1 and 3.2 from:
Daresh, J. (1988) *The pre-service preparation of American educational administrators: Retrospect and prospect.* Paper presented at the Research Meeting of the British Educational Management and Administration Society (BEMAS), Cardiff, Wales, April.

Figure 4.1 from:
Boyzatsis, R. (1982) *The Competent Manager: A model for effective performance.* New York: John Wiley.

Figure 7.1 from:
Sawatzki, M. (1997) 'Leading and managing staff for high performance', in B. Davies and L. Ellison (eds), *School Leadership for the 21st Century.* London: Routledge.

Figure 7.2 from:
Wilson, J., George, J., Wellins, R. and Byman, W. (1994) *Leadership Trapeze: Strategies for Leadership in Team-Based Organizations.* San Francisco: Jossey-Bass. Reprinted with permission of John Wiley & Sons, Inc.

1 | The nature of headship

So, you want to become an effective headteacher? Well, you face a challenge because as things stand we do not actually have a definition of what one looks like. Yes, we have aspirational models provided through images, metaphors and real-life practitioners and we even have published standards across the world that specify the tasks and personal qualities associated with formal school leadership, but none of these can be universally applied as each headship is unique. Headteachers are appointed to a school as well as to a system and the particular circumstances of that school are a major determinant of what an effective headteacher looks like as the role is context bound. Furthermore, headteachers occupy a key position in local society which means that the role has to be both active and reactive to the community the school serves. Headship is also a position of real authority, the pivotal position in the performance of the school and one that requires both an understanding of power and the ability to use it appropriately.

Typically people taking on a headship only come to understand the demands of the position some time after starting the job. For even the most hardened veteran of previous headships this usually takes at least six months and for first-time headteachers this can take several years, although most manage it within a two to three year period. This process of becoming effective takes so much time because you need to assimilate yourself to the demands of the job, the school as an organization, the community the school serves and the system in which the school operates. Effective headship, therefore, is the reconciliation of personal, organizational and systemic needs and aspirations. Usually this will mean reconciling personal, organizational, local and national agendas into an effective *gestalt* of activity.

Unfortunately we do not have templates for all aspects of headship. Nor do we have a secure theory base that is job specific. As will be demonstrated later in this chapter, the combination of regulations, contractual responsibilities and national and local cultures in England means that there are few similar positions to be seen in other school systems or occupations. Various

conversations that I have held over the years with colleagues have led me
to conclude that the nearest equivalent to headship is the captain of a ship
or aircraft. In that comparison we can see the captain as the person who has
immediate responsibility for determining action whilst remaining accountable to other stakeholders for the success of those decisions. In most
instances control of the craft and operating procedures are routine but vari-
ations in practice, especially those caused by the behaviour of the crew and
passengers, may require decision making without reference to higher
authority. This is a rare combination of accountability and responsibility
that I have not often seen mirrored in other school systems or occupations.
The nature of the job should have lent itself over time to the development
of a separate theory base for headship, but it hasn't. In the absence of such
a theory base we have attempted to substitute other theory bases and/or
make use of experiences from other occupations to shape the preparation,
support and continuing development of headteachers.

Theories Related to Headship

In trying to understand headship we have been dependent on the application
of theory from fundamental disciplines, such as psychology or sociology,
from applied theory, or from other types of organizations and school systems.
Leadership theory has the most currency at the beginning of the twenty-first
century, with the attendant implication that leadership and headship are one
and the same thing. Leadership theory is a highly contested conceptual field,
however, where little agreement is to be found amongst scholars, gurus, practitioners and policy makers. Multiple theories abound and the field is littered
with supposed holistic models of leadership which, when closely examined,
are actually contingent on context or circumstance.

Take the notion of Transformational Leadership, for example. First pro-
posed in the late 1970s, this model of leadership has attracted a legion of pro-
ponents and has been enthusiastically embraced by many who seek to
encourage change and development to individual behaviour within organizations. The basic idea is to gain commitment from members to the declared
or agreed aims of the organization. Once committed they engage more fully
and enthusiastically, accept greater levels of responsibility and move the
organization onwards and upwards in aspiration and performance.

The model is wholly contingent, however, on the willingness of the organizational members to personally engage with the organization or on the
skill of the formal leader to motivate them to such action. Trying to employ
the strategies associated with transformational leadership in an organization that is struggling or failing to meet its objectives is doomed to failure,
therefore, as the most effective and efficient leadership mode in those circumstances is actually transactional ("Do this and you will get that").

Leadership theories do not, of themselves, provide the answer to headship although they can provide some help and guidance (a theme we will return to later in this chapter). In trying to understand headship we need to accept the principle that although each headteacher position is ultimately a unique phenomenon, parallels for aspects of the job can be found in other formal leadership positions in differently focused organizations. We can see, therefore, that certain leadership behaviours will need to be exhibited by those in this pivotal role within a school and that school system.

Even so, we are still only looking at a very small part of the job. Any organization needs a combination of leadership, management and administration in order to run effectively and efficiently. In essence leadership is about decision making, choosing which path to follow, whilst management is about successfully following the chosen path and administration is about keeping the path tidy (Covey, 1992). The sets of behaviour that belong to each of those aspects of organizational operation are not so easily divisible in practice and are, of course, interdependent. Schools are similar in this way to other types of organization and those with formal responsibility need to engage in managerial or administrative activities (as well as leadership) or at least ensure that due attention is paid to those activities by capable others.

Effective headteachers achieve the right balance between leadership, management and administration both in terms of their personal engagement and the overall balance of those three operational aspects within the school. The centrality of any one set of behaviours is largely contingent on circumstance. Take, for instance, a school deemed to be in need of Special Measures following an external inspection. The required response in this type of situation will need to be largely managerial as there are many tried and trusted routes out of Special Measures. The need to engage in leadership behaviour in this situation is less important than ensuring good practice is encouraged in terms of lesson planning and behaviour management. This does not deny the importance of leadership for the long-term development of the school, as the ability to generate a vision, to encourage commitment and enrolment to that vision and to shape key strategic decisions remains integral to the role of the headteacher as formal leader. In the early days of Special Measures, however, managerial behaviour is more important with leadership behaviours generally being confined to interpersonal dimensions, such as the motivation of staff to sustain morale.

The conclusion made here is that effective headship is situational and contingent on context and circumstance. There is no commonly accepted theory of headship, although many theories contribute to the development of effective behaviour. Understanding the range of relevant theories, choosing from them according to need and applying them successfully to practice are major steps on the way to becoming an effective headteacher. Pulling these threads together may allow us to develop a coherent theory of headship that can inform the preparation, induction and development of headteachers.

The Nature of Headship

Effective headship, therefore, is the combination of leadership, managerial and administrative behaviours and actions that are appropriate to the given circumstance. Headteachers of highly effective schools tend to spend more of their time in the leadership mode, where decision making and influence are primary activities, than in the operational world where the emphasis is on a 'hands on' approach. This is not to say they do not engage in such mundane activities, merely that they effect most change through second order activity when they are the promoters and influencers rather than the 'doers'. Each and every school has multiple issues on a daily basis that require the head-teacher to be operationally focused. Maintaining a balance is key to this. Conversely, headteachers who are in schools with challenging circumstances will probably spend the major part of their time in operational rather than vision-ary mode, particularly in the early stages of improvement.

Effectiveness is judged, therefore, by outcomes. The definition of the desired outcomes is a matter for each school community to decide and I am not talking here of a simplistic model of effective schools that corresponds to student results on external tests. The entire range of effectiveness is, in effect, equal to the number of schools. In some state maintained schools, for example, the principal measure of effectiveness may be the student attendance rate; in others it may be the development of students who are independent learners. Whatever the context, the role of the headteacher is to assist the school community with the identification and achievement of agreed outcomes.

I should say here that there was great deliberation in the choice of the active verb for that last sentence, as too often aspirant headteachers are told, either implicitly or explicitly, that they are to be more deterministic than the words 'to assist' imply. It does not take a great deal of experience or imagination to see other verbs in operation such as 'direct' or 'lead'. Even worse, you can often detect the expectation that headteachers will not even work 'with' the school community, but will recruit others to their vision. This is the inherent danger of headship in that it carries with it societal and systemic expectations that confer greatness on the individual at the top of the organization. To help with the understanding of this phenomenon we need to look at the way in which formal leaders are perceived in different communities across the world.

The Effect of National Culture

People have a view of how they expect to interact with the 'boss' and this differs according to the culture. The work of Geert Hofstede, the Dutch social psychologist, on the influence of culture is very informative in this regard. Basing his work on the findings of anthropologists and social scientists (particularly Inkeles and Levinson, 1969), from the late 1960s and through the next decade he undertook a series of surveys that produced 117,000 responses from 88,000 employees from one world wide company (IBM). The only distinguishing variable between the respondents, he claimed, was their nationality. He suggested that nations, whilst not attaining the cohesiveness of isolated societies studied by field anthropologists, are still the source of a considerable amount of common mental programming of their citizens (Hofstede, 1980). The strong forces of common language, mass media, education systems, armed forces, political systems, sports and symbols add to this integration.

Hofstede investigated the perceptions of individuals on four issues: the relationship of individuals to authority; the relationship between the individual and the group; concepts of masculinity and femininity; ways of dealing with uncertainty. He found different solutions exhibited by IBM employees in the resolution of common problems that were largely determined by the dominant socialization processes evident in their country. From these data he was able to determine four dimensions that identified the differences between national cultures: *power-distance* (small to large); *collectivism* versus *individualism*; *femininity* versus *masculinity*; *uncertainty avoidance*.

Translating these into sets of national norms he was able to map how people from different countries were likely to react to these dimensions. The power-distance dimension allows for comparison between countries of dependence on bosses. The larger the gap, the more individuals are likely to accede to authority; the closer the gap, there will more likely be a desire for interdependence or independence. From his research he was able to identify the cultural characteristics of nation states. Little argument is likely to be seen between employees and bosses in Latin, Asian and African countries, he determined, whilst the converse is true in many European countries. Other dimensions demonstrate the way likely responses to problem solving will be resolved: in relation to the manner in which the society will value the contribution of individuals more than their contribution to a collective effort; whether basic social relationships accord to feminine or masculine mores; or how well people deal with the unknown.

From this analysis almost stereotypical models of preferred behaviours emerge. In the USA, for example, great emphasis is placed on the rugged individual, especially those exhibiting the characteristics of the frontiersmen, whilst German citizens tend to get very agitated when faced with uncertainty. The main features of the British state, the data suggested, are low to medium power-distance, low to medium uncertainty-avoidance, high individualism and high masculinity (as can be seen from Table 1.1).

Table 1.1   Country clusters and their characteristics

More developed Latin	Less Developed Latin	
High power-distance	High power-distance	
High uncertainty-avoidance	High uncertainty-avoidance	
Medium to high individualism	Low individualism	
Medium masculinity	Whole range on masculinity	
BELGIUM	COLOMBIA	
FRANCE	MEXICO	
ARGENTINA	VENEZUELA	
BRAZIL	CHILE	
SPAIN	PERU	
(ITALY)	PORTUGAL	

More developed Asian	Less Developed Asian	Near Eastern
Medium power-distance	High power-distance	High power-distance
High uncertainty-avoidance	Low to medium uncertainty-avoidance	High uncertainty-avoidance
Medium individualism	Low individualism	Low individualism
High masculinity	Medium masculinity	Medium masculinity
JAPAN		GREECE
	PAKISTAN	IRAN
	TAIWAN	TURKEY
	THAILAND	(YUGOSLAVIA)
	HONG KONG	
	INDIA	
	PHILLIPINES	
	SINGAPORE	

Germanic	Anglo	Nordic
Low power-distance	Low to medium power-distance	Low power-distance
Medium to high uncertainty-avoidance	Low to medium uncertainty-avoidance	Low to medium uncertainty-avoidance
Medium individualism	High individualism	Medium to high individualism
Medium to high masculinity	High masculinity	Low masculinity
AUSTRIA	AUSTRALIA	DENMARK
ISRAEL	CANADA	FINLAND
GERMANY	BRITAIN	NETHERLANDS
SWITZERLAND	IRELAND	NORWAY
	NEW ZEALAND	SWEDEN
	USA	
	(SOUTH AFRICA)	

Source: Hofstede (1980) cited in Pugh and Hickson (1989)

In his later work Hofstede was able to differentiate between workers within organizations in regard to their expectations of managers and leaders (Hofstede, 1994). He found significantly higher expectations that managers would demonstrate their authority from those with the lowest socio-economic status and level of educational achievement (generally the unskilled and semi-skilled workers), with a contrasting set of expectations from professional workers and co-managers.

Similar differences between national cultures have been recognized in other empirical research and contributions to the field (see for example Durcan, 1994; Trompenaars and Hampden-Turner, 1997). Durcan's research, for example, identified three clusters of countries within Europe that were characterized by similar values and patterns of behaviour which he labelled Anglo, Scandinavian and Mediterranean. The UK is placed within the Anglo cluster and is characterized by values and observations also observable in the USA, Canada, Australia and New Zealand. The Anglo culture focuses on results whilst leadership is seen as a means by which desired outcomes are achieved and the way in which a leader behaves toward followers in order to achieve results. The prevailing belief is that commitment (as opposed to compliance) of followers is to be secured by the formal leader doing more than merely exercising managerial authority. The leadership process not only includes good communication and human resource management strategies, therefore, but now also includes empowerment. Followers are motivated by challenges and opportunities whilst organizational structure is pragmatic, according to need.

The 'English' Factor

We need to go beyond this European view of Anglo cultures, however, if we are truly going to understand headship in England and take account of an 'English' factor which affects the mores and culture surrounding the schools in which they work. Being English is different from being British, although the latter includes the former.

Great Britain comprises, of course, the nation states of England, Scotland and Wales, whilst the United Kingdom also includes Northern Ireland. England is by far the biggest of the four countries with a population approximately seven times the size of the other three nations put together. Consequently the English and those in foreign climes still speak of Britain and England interchangeably, something the Welsh, Scots and Irish seldom do. Richards (1997) conducted an illuminating examination of the British character which, he suggested, was forged from Protestantism, empire, war with France, trade and parliamentary democracy. From that background comes the sense of duty, the famous British 'stiff upper lip', and individuality and tolerance – features that have been typically portrayed in mass media, particularly in the cinema. He identified two other specifically English characteristics, however, that create the distinctiveness of the English and their mainstream culture which contrast so markedly with the strong Celtic influence to be seen in the other British countries.

First, there is the sense of humour, considered a characteristic of the English since at least the Middle Ages. Pope Eugenius III declared in 1140 that the "English nation was fit to be set to anything it would handle and one to be preferred to others were it not for the impediment of levity". The second aspect is that ineffable sense of superiority. The Venetian ambassador reported in 1497: "The English are great lovers of themselves and of everything belonging to them. They think there are no other men like themselves and no other world but England".

My study of the field of national culture allowed me to previously apply these findings to England as part of an international study into the nature of formal school leadership and to identify a set of societal expectations for headship in England (Male, 1998). Most aspects of English society still generally expect a strong, individual character as headteacher, one who will encourage and tolerate debate from colleagues and other stakeholders and can operate, with gentle humour, within an environment where there is a great deal of uncertainty. Translating these findings into the everyday expectations of the formal school leader, most people will expect the headteacher in English schools to act as the 'boss' – albeit with a human touch – while teachers and other educationalists expect consultation and democracy from a professional colleague. Conversely, support staff and some parents may be more willing to rely on the headteacher as decision maker.

These expectations consequently affect the nature of interpersonal relationships between the headteacher and their school community. The position brings with it residual power. This is the power of office and one of the critical determinants of the nature of headship in England. Generally you will be expected to be 'the boss' and the likelihood is that people will start to treat you differently, sometimes transforming you into another entity without either your permission or knowledge. Take the example of these two headteachers, recounting their experience of becoming a headteacher. Firstly we hear from Richard, on becoming head of the school where he had been deputy for several years:

> You get treated differently and treat people differently. There is a natural unease in every teacher in relation to their head, regardless of how good, bad, or indifferent they are. People are cautious with you and, in turn, you can't behave in the way that maybe you would like to with them.

and Jane, talking about her relationships with the wider school community:

> People have a perception of you which changes when you are a headteacher. It's almost as though your face has changed, you're a different person.

Making the personal adaptation to cope with and master this change is the focus of the next chapter, but there is a need at this juncture to recognize the nature of headship that is inherent in the national culture and will almost certainly be reflected in the local and organizational social systems. The manifestation of the twin influences of culture and societal expectations frequently place the headteacher in an invidious, isolated position as they seek to satisfy society in general and their professional colleagues through their behaviour.

Is the Headteacher the Real School Leader?

Pragmatically, yes. Legally and theoretically, no.

Let me explain. Within the influence of national culture headteachers are perceived as the symbolic leader of the school, frequently as the personification of the school in action. This sensation of a 'head' is also supported by local and national systems that tend to see headteachers as the pivotal figure in terms of school performance. By the mid-1970s, for example, Her Majesty's Inspectorate (HMI) were reporting the quality of leadership as being the most influential factor in a school's success (Department of Education and Science, 1977). As headteachers were really the only ones heavily involved in school management at that time, the perception subsequently appeared that it was possible to substitute the word 'headship' for 'leadership' (a common, incorrect conclusion and, sadly, a view that is often still evident; see for example Hopkins, 2001).

Researchers, observers, practitioners and observers have added to this supposition that headteachers are the de facto leader, as well as manager, of the school. Heads 'feel' that 'the ultimate responsibility for everything that goes on lies with them' (Peters, 1976: 6), whilst others have viewed headship as 'pivotal' (Baron, 1968; House of Commons Select Committee,1998; Southworth, 2000). These findings and views of headship can be summed up as:

> The extraordinary centrality of the Headteacher in British schools. There is an almost universal focus of this job as being the pivot of all management and organization within schools ... We cannot think of any other established organization where this is the case, except perhaps the position of a British Prime Minister in relation to the Cabinet ... the nearest more ordinary comparison is with the founder–owner of a small business. (Torrington and Weightman,1989: 135–6)

The difficulty with these suppositions is that they deny the legal structures for the government and management of maintained schools, the contractual relationships of headteachers within the independent sector and the most effective models of formal leadership to be drawn from appropriate theory bases.

Headteacher Accountability

All headteachers are in a formal relationship with their employers, whether that be a public or private sector organization. For headteachers in the maintained sector the lines of accountability are blurred because of the seeming independence of the school in relation to the principal funding agency (usually the local authority who are also the employer). All maintained schools in England have their own governing body, each with their own articles and instruments of school government. The formal and legal responsibility for decision making within the maintained school lies with the governing body, therefore, rather than with the headteacher who is an employee of the principal funding agency. Equally in the independent sector you would normally find governors and/or trustees (in the event of the school being charitable in nature) who hold the ultimate responsibility for this same decision making and, in larger schools, the presence of a business manager (normally called the Bursar) who often has the same power and direct access to the employer as those enjoyed by the headteacher. To that end, therefore, headteachers cannot be described accurately as the 'head' any more than a managing director of a listed company working to the board of directors who, in turn, had been appointed by shareholders.

Headteachers in maintained schools do carry specific responsibility, however, for the internal organization, management and control of the school under the terms and conditions of employment contained within the School Teachers' Pay and Conditions Act 1991, and these alone make the job qualitatively different from any other in the state system of education. No other position has the same level of personal accountability with all major remaining positions being either collectively responsible (as is the case for governing bodies) or vicariously responsible under the terms of their employment. The notion of vicarious responsibility can be seen with teachers, for example, who cannot be held personally liable for negligence as it is the employer's responsibility to ensure the security of schooling for students. Headteachers are thus legally responsible for the internal, day to day issues within the school whilst governing bodies have strategic responsibility (see Figure 1.1).

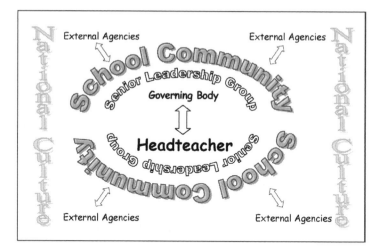

Figure 1.1 The typical relationship between stakeholders in English schools
© Trevor Male

The Role of the Governing Body

Governing bodies are often overlooked in the debate about headship, but they are an integral part of the complex system of checks and balances evident in the administration of public services. The principal purpose of such bodies is to address the concern society continues to exhibit over the prevention of fraud and misuse of public resources. Health services and the police, for example, have advisory or management boards that represent the interests of service users by including lay members in the governance of the provision, thus theoretically inhibiting the potential of service domination by professionals wielding expert power. In maintained schools the governing body is meant to play such a role through a mix of employer nominees, parent representatives, teachers and co-opted members who, through statute, collectively provide a measure of local accountability for the headteacher.

Headteachers are also full members of the governing body, but most often are the only education professional whose application to school leadership and management is full-time. The rhetoric of the law is that the governing body is the decision-making arm of the maintained school, responsible for setting policies and monitoring practice. In reality it is not common to find proactive governing bodies, however, principally because most members are part-time volunteers (Thody, 1998). Typically governing bodies are responsive to and supportive of headteacher initiative, although this assessment does not deny a continuum of practice ranging from political interference by members of the governing body in the day to day practice of the school, through to a total lack of interest by a group of press-ganged volunteers.

Headteacher time spent on governing bodies, however, is all too often about breathing life into the edifice rather than working with enthusiastic lay members of the public who are keen to act as para-professionals in the leadership and management of a school. The consequence is that headteachers are frequently required to play a much more deterministic role than that envisaged by the architects of school governance for the nation's maintained schools. Headship in reality, therefore, is commonly to be both the spiritual and pragmatic formal leader of a school.

The danger of this exposure is to make the position singular, an embodiment of the leader as hero innovator. Theoretically this is flawed, especially given what we know about higher order leadership skills and knowledge. Research into high-performing organizations demonstrates that the most appropriate formal leadership behaviours are those that allow the capabilities of others to flourish, whilst in situations of crisis or under-performance the converse is true. A high-performing organization is one that consistently outperforms similar or rival organizations over a significant period of time. There has been an array of organizations that have produced outstanding levels of performance in a particular age or circumstance, but few that can sustain these over time. A hugely popular book from a previous era, *In Search of Excellence* (Peters and Waterman, 1982), highlighted the key ingredients of successful organizations. It is a salutary lesson, therefore, to discover that over half the companies featured in that book have either gone into receivership or major decline since that time. To make the grade as an organization, to go from good to great, requires a level of sustained performance and formal leadership that consists of two key elements – *personal humility* and *professional will* (Collins, 2001).

This state of formal leadership is achieved through the paradoxical application of these twin elements. You have to know what you want, but you have to be big enough to recognize that you cannot achieve these objectives on your own. Furthermore, if you were to try you would almost certainly limit the range of possible solutions to the challenges facing your organization. Basically you do not know what you do not know, so if you set yourself up to be the answer to all questions then those will be the only answers you get. As Fullan (1993) puts it: 'premature vision and planning blind'.

The consequence is that effective headteachers build leadership capacity in their schools through encouraging others to develop vision and the processes that support the implementation of that vision into practice. The immutable part of that equation is the professional will of the formal leader, the strong personal desire for behaviours that correspond to the agreed values, principles and moral purpose that are to underwrite decision making and the actions that follow. Ultimately, effective headship is the manifestation of those values in practice and making full use of the opportunities and resources available. I will return to the identification, sustenance and possible modification of personal values in Chapter 3 and to the issue of building leadership capacity within the school in Chapter 7.

Towards a Theory of Headship

Attempts to describe the coordination of headteacher activity into effective practice have employed a number of theories and have even at times resorted to symbolism and mystique, with some contributors even suggesting that effective school leadership has a 'magic' quality. Nothing could be further from the truth. Formal school leadership involves both art and science and is a combination of behaviours that can be understood and learnt.

Firstly, we have already recognized that leadership theory is not sufficient in itself to explain headship in action, with management and administration being legitimate and complementary activities. The outcome of that discussion is that a model of contingency behaviour will be the recommendation. Consequently we have to explore the relevance of other theory bases, particularly those that have been drawn from fundamental subjects such as psychology, social psychology, anthropology and sociology. Fortunately many of the concepts drawn from these fields of study have already been applied to the study of leadership and management in action, but there is always a need to refer to the original sources when seeking understanding of our current context.

For the better part of the twentieth century the application of such theories was offered under the title of 'management' rather than 'leadership' and it was only at the close of the millennium that 'leadership' became the preferred term. Until that time leadership was often referred to as a sub-set of management theory, focused principally on the inter-personal aspects of the relation-ship between manager and employees. That style of relationship is perhaps best summed up in the description of the model offered by Sergiovanni (1992) who suggested that for the last half of the twentieth century we have consid-ered formal school leadership to be about two things: trying to figure out what needs to be done to make the school work and work well and trying to figure out how to get people to do these things. He labels this the 'expect and inspect' model which, on close examination, features only one aspect of lead-ership behaviour; the ability to keep up morale through the use of good human relations (see Table 1.2). This is, of course, a management model which has since been labelled 'managerial leadership' (Leithwood et al., 1999).

Table 1.2 The 'Expect and Inspect' model of school leadership

- State your objectives
- Decide what needs to be done to achieve these objectives
- Translate these work objectives into role expectations
- Communicate these expectations
- Provide the necessary training
- Put the people to work
- Monitor the work
- Make corrections when needed
- Throughout, practise human relationships leadership to keep morale up

Source: Sergiovanni (1992)

Managerial leadership has its place in the pantheon of possible behaviour patterns to be offered by headteachers. In a school system where organiza-tional structures and processes are largely pre-defined, such a model would be close to an ideal behaviour pattern for the formal school leader. In the USA, for example, where the officers of the school district, particularly the superintendent, play a dominant role in relation to the organization, content and delivery of the schooling process, the school principal is best advised to adopt the model of managerial leadership. All too often the only alternative would be to engage in conflict and political activity, for which they will need a secure power base in order to survive.

Arguably there has been widespread application of this model of manage-rial leadership by headteachers in England, particularly since the introduc-tion of a national inspection system in 1992. Indeed, one well-placed observer judged the requirements of the external inspection process by the Office for Standards in Education (Ofsted) to have become the dominant model of school effectiveness by the late 1990s (Bolam, 1997). There is even an argument to suggest that the model is still evident in the National Profes-sional Qualification for Headship (NPQH), but more of that in Chapter 4!

For schools in the twenty-first century, however, there is much more freedom to choose their course of action, especially for those schools which are not causing concern to central or local government agencies, so leadership is often a much greater need than managerial activity. For *leadership* to occur you have to have *followers*, not just subordinates; to be an effective leader you have to have a number of colleagues who share the same commitment as you and do not just go along with you because you are 'the boss'. Managerial leadership does not rely on this level of commitment and can operate successfully in a climate of compliance.

Senge (1990) draws a distinction between being *enrolled* in a process, of becoming part of something by choice, and being *committed*, described as being not only enrolled, but feeling fully responsible for making the vision happen. He makes the point that in most organizations there are relatively few enrolled and even fewer committed: most are in a state of compliance. Genuinely compliant colleagues will go along with the leaders of the organization because they can see the benefits and do everything expected and more, whilst others will be less enthusiastically inclined and will continue to participate either because they know no better or because it is too difficult to mount a challenge to the driving force. Some organizational members may, of course, refuse to comply because they hold different views or are merely apathetic.

The distinction between genuine compliance and enrolment, therefore, is the difference between 'accepting' the vision and 'wanting' the vision. For a school to be successful you need the committed, the enrolled and the genuinely compliant to combine in order to achieve a critical mass of aligned power that drives leadership activity in support of the declared aims.

The conclusion here is that there is a continuum of activity that encompasses effective headship, with relevant models of management and leadership being contingent on local circumstances. The single thing that differentiates headship from other formal managerial or leadership positions is the high level of personal accountability for a client-focused service 'owned' by multiple stakeholders. Effective headteachers need, therefore, a battery of leadership, management and administrative theories at their disposal from which they can draw relevant skills and behaviours to match the needs of their school community. The exact match will be a unique combination as no two circumstances are the same, yet all the time the headteacher has to remain aware of the risk they run in relation to decision making in a political environment. This is the closest we can come to theory of headship.

The Pathway to Effective Headship

There are many discernible stages in attaining effective headship, as you will see in the chapters that follow, but the key dividing factors are preparation, induction and consolidation. Beginning headteachers are now better prepared than ever before, with licensure schemes such as the NPQH ensuring at least exposure of aspirant headteachers to a relevant body of knowledge and to the development of a basic skills set appropriate to the demands of the job. All headteachers have to enter organizations, however, as both the newest member and the most influential one, a process that will be aided by focused preparation and effective induction procedures. Once the shock of entry recedes, the effective headteacher sets out to engage in the higher order skills of leadership, a pathway that may take many years to achieve if it is achieved at all. The first steps along the way are likely to be uncertain, confusing and challenging but research shows that most seem to make it through to become a successful incumbent in time.

One aim of this book is to make that path a little smoother as we can anticipate many of the challenges to be faced. Those headteachers who successfully make it through the preparation and induction phases can then enter a period of consolidation where original ideas and aspirations are worked through to some level of fruition. Effective headteachers can then go on to seek extension beyond that plateau into the high plains of leadership, where the full capability and potential of members of a school community are developed in support of the student body it serves.

At this level headteachers become less obvious and their behaviour goes almost unnoticed as colleagues, empowered both by their liberation and their own abilities, take immediate responsibility for decision making and leadership activity. The headteacher operating at this level is thus a facilitator rather than a controller, guiding people rather than directing them. The best analogy I can come up with is engine oil. Very few remember the oil in their car engine, yet without it the engine would very quickly seize up. Engines will run for a short time without oil, as will a school without an effective headteacher, but both will grind to a halt sooner or later without that subtle influence, perhaps best described by the Chinese philosopher Lau-Tzu, who said:

> As for the best leaders, the people do not notice their existence. The next best, the people honour and praise. The next, the people fear: and the next the people hate. When the best leader's work is done, the people say "We did it ourselves". (Cited in Katzenbach and Smith, 1994)

So your pathway to effectiveness culminates in becoming invisible! Not a viable destination for egotists, but one that leads to the best results for the student body you seek to serve.

2 | The transition to formal leadership

The transition to formal school leadership contains a number of required learning experiences that mainly need to be accumulated during your working life, although they may also be configured by personal attributes or a personal history that has taken on board the relevant experiences in an unconscious, unplanned manner. It is my contention that, even with the formal requirement of licensure schemes such as NPQH, headteachers are not fully prepared for the position through prior training or experience and, consequently, require access to a range of development activities and support before appointment and during induction that will make them more effective in their new job.

That belief has been established as a result of previous research I had carried out, singly and jointly in the UK and the USA, since before the beginning of the NPQH programme and the publication of national standards for headteachers (Male, 1996; Daresh and Male, 2000; Male and Merchant, 2000). That body of research had produced data that suggested that beginning headteachers were not fully prepared for the job, particularly in being able to deal with the transition to a formal leadership position that was integral to the concept of the post, findings that were also reflected in similar, contemporary studies (Dunning, 1996; Draper and McMichael, 1998). These are views I continue to hold despite regular changes to the content and structure of national standards and the NPQH.

The general trend of the literature and research on the transition to become the formal leader of an organization is that in order to be successful the new postholder must have a range of personal capabilities and skills sufficient for the demands of the job. Particularly helpful in the framing of this transition from aspirant to practising formal leader are the conclusions of Gronn (1993) who, in studies of leadership succession, developed a four stage model that begins with Formation, passes through Accession to Incumbency and finally ends with Divestiture. During the formative stage the future leader is subject to a range of early influences from agencies such as the family, school and other reference groups which shape their personality as a leader. During accession to the post, the prospective leader makes progress to their future position through the creation of appropriate knowledge and expertise. In some instances this is a planned accession by the individual, but it may also be a path that is unplanned with the prospective leader not necessarily recognizing themselves as a putative postholder during the learning process. The period of incumbency covers the total length in time of the post, from appointment to leaving. Divestiture covers the leaving period for those retiring or the disenchanted, or a time of re-invention for the enchanted.

It is possible to use this leadership literature and theory base to predict some of the challenges faced by school leaders as they move from a state of anticipation about the new job to the point where they feel confident and competent in their new post. In other words they will have managed the process of transition in order to have become effective. The case was strongly made in the previous chapter, however, that the nature of headship made it a qualitatively different experience than formal leadership in other organizations and school systems. Fundamental to that argument was the rare combination of personal accountability and societal expectations that provides the headteacher with few refuges in the maelstrom of activity that typically surrounds the post.

Making the transition to this formal leadership position introduces a number of challenges that arise in addition to having accumulated the requisite skills base to be judged a potentially effective headteacher. These challenges permeate the period of preparation, induction and early stages of consolidation in the new post and affect every newly appointed headteacher, irrespective of their previous experience. Although we can learn much from the literature and research concerning the succession of leaders, managers and administrators in general, moving to a headship position thus brings with it a unique set of circumstances relating not only to occupational expectations or standards but also to the personal and organizational dimensions of the transition. This chapter explores those three dimensions and will guide you toward an understanding that will be relevant to your specific context.

The Personal Dimension

The personal dimension of headship preparation and induction relates largely to the issues of reconciling your self-image and preferred behaviours with the demands of the post. Newly appointed headteachers undertake a journey of discovery about themselves and, in contrast to the other two dimensions, often find that this aspect of the transition can leave them isolated and lonely. Whilst these feelings are more marked in first-time head-teachers, there is still enough evidence from studies on career transition to show that all headteachers find the challenges of the new job cause them to re-evaluate their image of self.

My research in this field demonstrates that the key issues for the preparation of first-time headteachers are the formation of attitudes and values and the need for differentiated development activities according to previous experience, gender, ethnicity and age. Meanwhile, the early stages of headship are accompanied by feelings of surprise, isolation and loneliness. In addition, there is a common need to divest previous attributes and behaviours in favour of new ones more appropriate to the demands of headship resulting in a period of cognitive dissonance in relation to an understanding of the self. The evidence tends to demonstrate changed behaviour patterns by those moving into headship that frequently affect personal and social life, particularly for those who find themselves to be in a more challenging position than they had anticipated when applying for the job.

The Organizational Dimension

The organizational dimension, largely informed by socialization theory, highlights issues related to understanding the culture of the organization, including recognizing the influence of the previous incumbent and encouraging the exploration of alternative structures and systems as a new headteacher begins to influence the culture of a school. Central to these issues is the need for acceptance and the support of existing staff, particularly more senior members.

The Occupational Dimension

The occupational dimension focuses on the generic issues relating to the adaptation required by the aspirant headteacher to become effective in post. This includes the development of a range of skills in the preparation stage, with the probable need for differentiation according to the phase or type of school, and for that preparation to provide a range of learning activities appropriate to the reality of the job in action. During accession and the early stages of incumbency, there is a need for support systems that will allow beginning headteachers to explore their values in relation to the job as experienced and to recognize the staged development of their occupational identity. Such support systems are likely to include mentoring and networking with peers and more experienced colleagues to explore and resolve dilemmas and challenges emerging at a personal or organizational level.

Routes to Effective Headship

The newly appointed headteacher thus has two routes to follow when first appointed: the occupational and the personal/organizational. These are pictured in Figure 2.1 below and clearly show the different issues to be faced before the first stage of successful headship is reached, that point where an incoming headteacher feels confident and competent in their new job. The occupational route is well populated, busy and closely focused on matching the incoming headteacher to the anticipated demands of the school system, whilst the personal/organizational route is lonely and indeterminate as the unique demands of both job and school emerge. Both routes have to be followed, but it is only when these come together that the headteacher can become strategic. From that initial high point of competence and confidence those in search of effective headship can strike out for the high plains of team working and distributed leadership which signify your final destination.

Moving into Headship

Research into headship has demonstrated that few are prepared for the demands of the position to which they are appointed, with this statement holding true for second or subsequent headships. The nature of the challenge in such circumstances is clearly different, but there is ample evidence emerging to demonstrate that success in one school does not necessarily ensure success in a subsequent post. The experience of so-called 'super heads' appointed to Fresh Start schools in England during the last days of the twentieth century provides a graphic example of the difficulties of transition from one headship to another, with only a couple of those originally appointed being able to effect real and lasting change in their new and challenging environments. Similarly, recent research into second headships has demonstrated how difficult it is for a headteacher to be continually successful in subsequent schools (MacKenzie, 2005).

First-time headteachers, meanwhile, are initially shocked both by the intensity of the job and the relentless demands on them to address challenging and seemingly intractable problems (see for example Draper and McMichael, 1998; Daresh and Male, 2000). Typical of recent participants in my surveys into beginning headship are some comments by two primary school headteachers, who point out that "none of us is prepared for headship" and "no amount of training prepares you for the actual total responsibility of the job".

Headship as a Unique Occupation

So what are the essential differences that make headship unique in its demands? First is the individual exposure provided by the combination of legal, systemic and societal demands that sets headteachers apart from others in formal decision-making positions within the school system. As

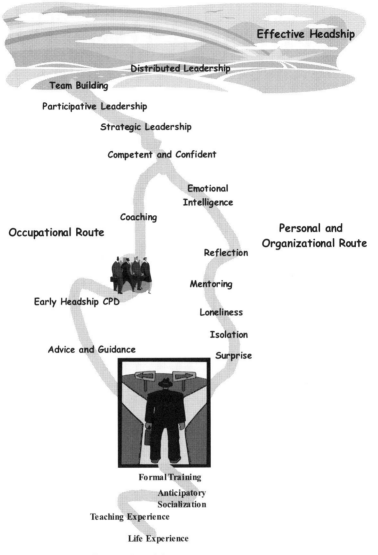

Effective Headship

Distributed Leadership

Team Building

Participative Leadership

Strategic Leadership

Competent and Confident

Emotional Intelligence

Coaching

Occupational Route

Reflection

Personal and Organizational Route

Mentoring

Early Headship CPD

Loneliness

Isolation

Advice and Guidance

Surprise

Formal Training

Anticipatory Socialization

Teaching Experience

Life Experience

Figure 2.1   Routes to effective headship
© Trevor Male

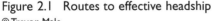

the symbolic and pragmatic leader within the school community, a head-teacher thus makes the transition from anonymity or vicarious responsibility in their previous job to personal accountability in their new one. This type of accountability is not as evident in other organizations or school systems across the world, thus making comparisons difficult.

Second is the requirement to make the mid-career transition to a job that bears very little resemblance to initial training. Although there are some claims that the experiences of teaching can contribute to success in headship, there are enormous parts of the job for which there exists no discernible, transferable skills (Draper and McMichael, 1998). Similarly, responses from participants in my research demonstrate they consider being a headteacher to be very different from being a teacher. All leadership and management processes involve the achievement of objectives with and through others and are thus second order activities. The learning experiences needed for this type of behaviour are not evident in initial training, nor have they been a central feature of teaching where typically most change has been effected through first order relationships. Until the advent of formal qualifications for headship, prospective headteachers tended to learn these new skills and required behaviours through in-service education, particularly through work experience.

Third is the need to assimilate yourself into a school where not only are you the new member of staff, but you are also viewed as the pivotal figure in any future success for the institution. There is no quarter offered to beginning headteachers who are expected, and have often been specifically appointed, to add to the quality of the school. All too often no opportunity is offered to take stock, to become familiar with the particular circumstances and issues that are important to your new school community and to evaluate a range of options for action. This is unfortunate as we know only too well the adage that decisions made in haste can be repented at leisure.

Very few people, however, seem prepared to give a new headteacher time to demonstrate their capability and expect some early evidence of their readiness for the job. The longer you go without providing that evidence, the quicker any honeymoon period of headship will evaporate. This is an unrealistic expectation and is in contradiction to the evidence base that suggests the early days in any new leadership post are about 'making sense' of the new situation (Gabarro, 1987; Reeves et al. 1998; Weindling, 2000), a period of transition successfully expressed by one of my respondents: "it is only after about 6 months in the job that you begin to appreciate what you don't know".

Fourth is the need to overcome the feelings of isolation and inadequacy that accompany headship. Making the transition to headship requires a transformation in views of the self and a coming to terms with how others perceive you. The process can be deemed complete when you feel both comfortable and confident in the position, a process that can take months or years depending on the local circumstances you find in the school to which you are appointed. Headteachers perceive themselves to be most effective when they have reconciled their image of themselves at work with their personal self-image. This is a psychodynamic approach that is best described as the 'reconciliation of situational self with substantial self' (Nias, 1989). In layman's terms this is when you are acting in similar fashion both at work and at home (or play).

In the early stages of a first headship, beginning headteachers often search for an identity that will convey their authority and will model their behaviour to mirror others they have seen in that role. Subsequently they adapt and modify this behaviour in order that it is aligned more closely to their beliefs, values, thinking styles and preferred behaviours (Mahony, 2004). Those entering their second or subsequent headships are often more confident in their sense of self, yet can still find themselves struggling to sustain their preferred patterns of behaviour in this new social system. The processes of adaptation and modification that follow are the reconciliation of their situational self, frequently based on role adoption, and their substantial self, which is their natural way of behaving.

In other words, effective headteachers are able to act and think at work in their preferred individual (and sometimes idiosyncratic) ways. Some people believe that the substantial self is formed through affective individual learning experiences and processes that are relatively impervious to change. This cannot be true, however, as the substantial self is almost always affected by work situations and a headship may be a major factor in the re-alignment of personal self-image. That is not the main issue, however, as it is the reconciliation of the two images that is evident in effective headteachers.

These four factors represent powerful claims for the unique nature of the post and provide reasons for considering the transition to headship as being of a different order and intensity than to formal leadership in other occupations and school systems. Despite these claims, however, many similarities can still be seen between headship and formal leadership and it is that knowledge, coupled with focused research into beginning headship, which allows us to draw some parallels and to anticipate many of the issues that will accompany the career transition to headship.

The Transition to Formal Leadership

Aspects of socialization theory are most commonly used to explain the succession to formal leadership and Barnett (2001) points to the way this knowledge base has been touted as a means of distinguishing between the aspects of personal development that relate to joining an organization and the adoption of an occupational identity. Most commentators make use of Merton's (1968) definition of socialization:

> The process by which people selectively acquire the values, attitudes, the interests, skills and knowledge – in short the culture – current in groups to which they are, or seek to become, a member.

'Socialization', however, is one of the vaguest terms employed in the vocabulary of the social sciences and has included descriptors drawn from a number of other disciplines, including psychology, sociology and anthropology (Brezinha, 1994). Merton's definition corresponds mostly to social situations, has been interpreted narrowly in examining issues relating to entering headship and is described as having two aspects: 'professional' and 'organizational' (Weindling, 2000). 'Organizational socialization' is defined as the process by which one learns the knowledge, values, and behaviours required to perform a specific role within a particular organization (Schein, 1988). 'Professional socialization', on the other hand, attempts to describe the process which involves learning what it is to be a headteacher, becoming familiar with the real and potential power and authority associated with the position and adopting the mantle of 'boss' within the school community. A person begins to learn this prior to taking up the job, from their own experience of schooling and teaching as well as through formal courses, but organizational socialization can only, by definition, begin after taking up the post.

Professional Socialization

Whilst useful as a descriptor of the process of adaptation to an occupational identity, particularly to a senior role in a social organization, 'professional socialization' is an imprecise definition by which to describe the transition to effective headship. Attempts to explore the development and support needed for the transition to headship have drawn on a number of other occupations where high-level decision making in relation to other humans is a requisite part of the job. Daresh (1995), for example, explored law, medicine and training for the priesthood, searching for possible lessons for the development and support of future principals in the USA. Eraut (1994) talked of professional knowledge and competence but used a wider field of alternative occupations, taking account of what he calls 'semi-professions' which do not have the range of traits associated with the so-called 'ideal' professions of medicine and law.

Studies such as these remain inappropriate to headship for several reasons, principally on the grounds that until the introduction of the NPQH licensure scheme there had been no formal requirement to prepare for headship and, furthermore, it is a mid-career development that requires a different range of knowledge and behaviours than those needed to enter teaching as a career. In contrast, members of the 'ideal' professions undertake vocationally-oriented studies prior to entering the job as do most, if not all, of the occupations that could claim to be called 'professions'. Whilst it is possible to draw some parallels with other careers, the fundamental difference is that headteachers do not necessarily begin their career with headship in mind. All pre-qualified doctors, for example, expect to become doctors in time and so can manage the transition into the job in line with the development of their knowledge base and competence, whereas few may have anticipated becoming managers of health-care practices.

Elsewhere Weindling (2000) makes use of professional socialization to describe the transition to headship and argues that is can be learnt, at least in part, prior to taking up the role. This has been described as a process of 'anticipatory socialization' whereby the prospective postholder prepares themselves through gathering social and technical experiences that will qualify them for the role (Taylor, 1968; Greenfield, 1985; Eraut, 1994). Most discussion of anticipatory socialization is posited on the notion that this is a deliberate process by upwardly mobile aspirants, but Merton draws attention to this process having the propensity to be both conscious and unconscious. In his discussion of anticipatory socialization, he states:

> Conducing to this stage of anticipatory socialization is the structural circumstances of what can be called role gradations. The individual moves more or less continuously through a sequence of statuses and associated roles, each of which does not differ greatly from the one which has gone before. (Merton, 1968: 239)

These gradations serve as an informal preparation that may go unnoticed by the individual performer at the time. In short, it may be an unconscious process that brings the individual to a position where there is a high likelihood of acquiring some of the values and orientations associated with new, but related, roles and statuses (Greenfield, 1977).

Although Greenfield's work at that time was not tested empirically, the hypothesis bears a striking similarity to the way in which teachers pass through a number of graded roles on route to headship (Daresh and Male, 2000) and may go some way to explaining how some beginning headteachers appear to have assimilated a comprehensive range of technical and personal skills and capabilities without necessarily engaging in a formal programme of occupationally focused training and development. Whilst it is inevitably true that some teachers enter the school system with ambitions to be a headteacher, and thereby systematically prepare themselves in terms of knowledge and experience appropriate to the anticipated job, there is nothing inherent in their preparation as teachers that would lead to that conclusion. Not all of the qualities that make them successful as a teacher, therefore, will automatically transfer to headship.

Notwithstanding this, any use of the notion of professional socialization as the theory base that explains the succession to headship still has an attractiveness, as it can be demonstrated to cover the periods of formation, accession and the early days of incumbency, thus covering the time both prior to achieving an occupational identity as well as that during situational adjustment when newcomers take on the characteristics required by the situation in which they participate, some of which are contingent on earlier life experiences (Becker, 1964). Greenfield (1985) provides a useful perspective on the pre-entry stage of the career transition when he makes a distinction between the 'technical' and 'moral' socialization undertaken in preparation. He defines moral socialization as the development of attitudes, values and beliefs required for adequate performance in role, whilst technical socialization is concerned with the development of knowledge and behaviour that reflects technical, conceptual and social skills and activities associated with role enactment. The combination of these two socialization processes, he argues, provides individuals with the knowledge, ability and dispositions needed for performance in role.

Organizational Socialization

Discussion conducted on the transition to headship through socialization has focused, so far, on the processes by which an individual comes to terms with the demands of a job – in this case as a headteacher. An over-emphasis on formal leaders as single, self-conscious and self-actualized people, however, runs the risk of missing major components of the succession process (Weaver-Hart, 1993). There is a specificity to headship that moves it beyond the generic field, in that each appointment is to a school rather than a system. The dynamics of becoming a part of that organization are complex and interactive; to take on the mantle of formal leader for the same organization is even more complicated. Socialization theory, in this instance organizational socialization, has again been used to explain the process and to assist newcomers with effecting successful transitions to the job of formal leader of a school.

A large body of work exists on this aspect of the socialization process where previous writers have suggested stage theories to explain aspects of transition experienced by formal school leaders. Weaver-Hart (1993), for example, made an extensive theoretical and empirical study of principals in the USA entering their new jobs that illustrated the range of influences that shaped the position. In completing the study, she drew on the concept of organizational socialization to examine the effects on leaders and organizations from various directions, recognizing that leader successors are newcomers who must be integrated into existing groups, validated by social processes and granted legitimacy by subordinates and superiors before they can have significant impacts on actions taken by others. Her work allowed her to emphasize the two-way interaction between a new leader and their organization and to delineate a three-stage process of Encounter, Adjustment and Stabilization. The encounter or arrival stage begins immediately after appointment and demands a steep learning curve on the part of any new leader regarding the social setting of the school. The second stage of adjustment involves the task of fitting in. A new leader must reach an accommodation with the work role, the people with whom he or she interacts and the existing school culture. More stable patterns begin to emerge in the third stage by which time new leaders would have resolved conflicts about how their approach fits into the organization and will have located themselves within the context.

Whilst there is much to be learned from the Weaver-Hart study, there are differences between the nature of headship in England and the nature of principalship in the USA which must be considered. Headteachers have much more in the way of direct responsibility than their American counterparts. Principals are appointed to a system – the school district – and have a direct, upward, line-management relationship with a superintendent. It is not uncommon to find a principal being appointed to a school by the superintendent and for the same principal to serve at that level in several schools within the same district. Governance is at a district rather than school level, with an elected school board taking responsibility for all the schools in that district.

These governance and management structures contrast with those to be found in England which are far more localised. English headteachers in state-maintained schools, for example, often find it difficult to nominate their 'superior' in the system and when asked to choose are torn between the governing body and the chief education officer of the local authority. In consequence many of the issues referred to by Weaver-Hart regarding relationships with 'superiors' are only either tangentially relevant or largely irrelevant when using her work to understand the transition to headship.

In pointing out, however, that first-time principals experience a double socialization experience – professional socialization to school leadership and organizational socialization to their immediate work setting (Weaver-Hart, 1993) – she does provide us with an important lens through which we can view the transition to headship. The essential difference is the way in which an incoming principal or headteacher is viewed by those with whom they work most closely. To make the transition successful, the incoming headteacher must either satisfy the expectations of the school community or be able to adjust and shape their new colleagues' expectations through changing the criteria by which they are to be judged.

Socialization Tactics

Van Maanen (1978) demonstrates that individuals, organizations and systems apply a number of tactics, consciously or unconsciously, to influence the integration of new members. The tactics employed by the incoming individual are related to their perceived status in the organization, with those destined for the formal leadership position being placed in the unique situation of both influencing and being influenced as they make the transition. This recognition leads, in turn, to the identification of different stages of capability, often defined by a period of time, according to the way in which the individual and the existing social system make mutual adjustments to accommodate each other's preferences.

Typically the collective that is the organization or system seeks to assimilate the newcomer into its existing mores and patterns of behaviour.

Acceptance of such a custodial response would lead to few changes in behaviour as the inherited past would continue to dominate at both the individual and organizational level, leaving the new leader looking much the same as their predecessor (Weaver-Hart, 1993). This, however, is the natural response of the collective which tends, as a social group, to be conservative in nature. But a new leader with a different perspective, belief or objectives may seek to change and innovate.

Leaders appointed on such a mandate may work either within existing systems and values, seeking only tactical changes to achieve higher levels of success, or they may try to effect radical change by rejecting many of the established norms and even by redefining the ends as well as the means. Whichever approach is taken there will be a different set of learning experiences for the leader as they enter the job, make adjustments to their new circumstances and establish themselves in a new role. There is no universal truth to the way in which this process will manifest itself and no specific route map available prior to taking up post. There are general rules of engagement and tools of analysis available, however, which can provide greater understanding of the individual position during the transition period.

The Stages of Transition

Factors relating to the transition to formal leadership have been placed into three categories of Context, Content and Sociality through the work of Jones (1986). He made use of the socialization tactics identified by Van Maanen and Schein (1978) who had established the paired comparisons of the collective or individual; formal or informal; sequential or random; fixed in time or variable; serial or disjunctive; investiture or divestiture. By making use of these paired comparisons in relation to the context, content and social aspects of leadership succession, it is possible for a new leader to map their specific circumstance and predict some of the experiences they are likely to meet during the early stages of their induction (see Table 2.1).

In terms of the context, Jones (1986) meant that the transition to the lead-

Table 2.1 Socialization tactics

Context	Collective	v	Individual
	Formal	v	Informal
Content	Sequential	v	Random
	Fixed	v	Variable
Sociality	Serial	v	Disjunctive
	Investiture	v	Divestiture

Adapted from Van Maanen and Schein (1978)

ership position is either collective or individual and formal or informal. The content (meaning that learning required) is either sequential or random and fixed or variable, while the social processes are either serial (that is, with role models) or disjunctive and involve investiture or divestiture. These three categories of socialization tactics can be applied to all stages of the transition to formal leadership, including the period of anticipatory socialization.

Those preparing for leadership or entering a new organization or system, therefore, may do so either *collectively* as a group of people or *individually.* Individuals develop their capability, a range of skills and the personal qualities on which they draw *formally* or *informally.* Where the preparation and/or induction is conducted collectively, similar messages can be imparted which can shape their future response as leaders to organizationally-based issues. Alternatively, group preparation and induction can result in the individual members being able to draw on a collective authority that allows them to sustain individual values and beliefs within a new social system. Nationally or locally then, it may be possible for the appropriate agency to prepare and induct new leaders in such a way as to diminish the custodial effect of the organization. Collective preparation and induction can thus impart a systemic need over (latent) organizational desire and we can see evidence of this in licensure programmes such as the NPQH and with induction programmes run nationally, such as HIP, or locally by independent trusts, local authorities or a diocese.

We can even see an occupational dimension to this with regard to professional associations and bodies, each of whom have a perspective on their members' behaviour and have established codes of practice and accompanying disciplinary procedures. An example of this type of group coherence can often be seen amongst those who have worked together in their development towards headship, such as members of a NPQH cohort. In this case members can often be seen to maintain contact with each other or meet regularly, using the strength of their relationships to share common issues of concern which will help them to resolve individual issues.

Headship is ultimately an individual occupation, however, and the newly appointed headteacher will be more frequently subject to the latent socialization power of the organization or school system than if they join a group. Here the danger is that the new arrival has no common, internal reference point. Thus the message in preparing to enter headship is fairly straightforward, in that the beginning headteacher needs a support network that extends beyond the school community to which they are appointed.

Headteacher Induction

Similarly the induction may be formal or informal. In other words the organization or system may have a planned series of events *(formal),* although this is seldom the case and most leadership transition is under-taken informally. Numerous studies of early headship show planned induc-tion for headteachers of state-maintained schools to be spasmodic in intensity, with no comparative data available for the independent sector. During the 1980s, for example, a major study of early headship in England found that just one quarter of newly appointed headteachers received any formal induction, inevitably run by the local authority, which lasted more than one day (Weindling and Earley, 1987).

By the middle of the next decade there had been some improvement as a result of two government funded schemes to support the early stages of headship. The first of these, the Headteacher Mentoring Scheme, made a significant impact in the two years it ran before the funding was effectively withdrawn in order to support more general leadership and management development activities (Bolam et al., 1993). By the end of the decade, however, the majority of first time headteachers had registered for HEAD-LAMP, a government sponsored induction programme that supported their development during the first two years in post. With most LEAs registered as providers, headteachers in state-maintained schools tended to receive a formal programme of induction as LEAs were the dominant market force in the development of beginning headteachers.

A subsequent review of headteacher induction was critical of LEAs' efforts, however, indicating that no programmes were considered to be 'very good' (Office for Standards in Education, 2002). The LEA induction programmes, they found, failed to differentiate effectively for headteachers from different schooling phases and where there was good practice it was inconsistently applied. Furthermore, engagement by beginning headteachers was variable.

Whilst all LEAs provided basic information about the HEADLAMP scheme there was not much monitoring and evaluation of individual head-teacher's spending or of its impact on a headteacher's capacity to take a school forward. About a quarter of headteachers had made no firm deci-sions about how to spend HEADLAMP money to best effect, with many reporting a lack of information about providers and courses. Consequently most headteachers spent the HEADLAMP money on a mixed programme of support and courses, from LEAs, universities and private consultants.

When HEADLAMP was withdrawn in 2003 and replaced with the Head-teacher Induction Programme (or HIP), the situation actually worsened for headteachers in maintained schools in England as LEAs were no longer able to be providers, the NCSL instead appointing just 20 providers nationally (later reduced to 12). In consequence not only did local authorities typi-cally no longer support first-time headteachers, but they also found it diffi-cult to support the induction of any headteacher new to their school system. With such a high portion of their overall expenditure having to be delegated directly to schools, local authorities struggled to provide some services, even when they were deemed statutory responsibilities (such as headteacher induction).

In many instances, therefore, the quality of the induction processes for LEAs was questionable, with a tendency for administrative and legal responsibilities to dominate the agenda at the expense of personal development and organizational change. It was a 'sink or swim' process of socialization for most in this regard. Good practice, where it was clearly visible, included good early contacts and good introductory meetings, support from link advisers and clear, relevant identification of needs that were specific to both headteacher and school. Where established, networks of headteachers, particularly those meeting in phase groups, provided valuable support on the more wide-ranging aspects of headship. Link advisers' support was similarly valuable in most LEAs and in all phases, often because the focus of a visit was jointly agreed and specific to headteachers' and the schools' needs.

Whilst these criteria provide a template for a model of transition, the status, funding and intent of employers has generally meant newly appointed headteachers have been forced to manage their own learning through the early stages of a new career. As my research has shown, most have successfully achieved this task in an informal manner including – for the vast majority of those appointed to headship before the introduction of the compulsory NPQH in England – the management of their own preparation informally.

Whilst their resourcefulness and resilience are to be applauded, this is no way to run a national system. But given the lack of intermediary agencies, this may be the only route to successfully managed transitions to headship in England for the forseeable future, especially as HIP has had a troubled birth and is still struggling to achieve coherence at the time of writing.

Knowledge Building

The management of learning in relation to the content or appropriate body of knowledge needed during the transition to formal leadership varies according to the type of job. Where events are predictable, appropriate knowledge can be imparted at the most opportune time (*sequential*). Conversely, the situation may be so fluid, so ambiguous and so rapidly changing that the induction experience becomes informal and *random*. The timetable for successful transition may also be *fixed* or *variable*.

Some leadership positions, for example, are probationary with tenure judged on capability being demonstrated during a given time frame. Principals in the Chicago Public School system, for example, have a four year renewable contract under the terms of their 1988 Reform Act which means they have to be judged as effective or capable by the third year at least if they are to retain their post. From what we know of headship we can conclude the post is more likely to be random in nature and variable in length. Incoming headteachers will invariably be exposed to knowledge on a need-to-know basis, with such a potential outcome sitting well within the 'sense-making' period illustrated above. Few patterns are predictable in the first year of tenure whilst a newly appointed headteacher is building local knowledge, with subsequent years being affected principally by the vagaries of policy makers. In the absence of a probationary period or fixed term appointments, the new headteacher's successful transition is again subject to local circumstance.

The outcome is that headteacher learning is largely informal and random, with no clear indication or expectation of when the 'honeymoon' period will be over and at what stage the harsh reality of judgement will begin against them. Thus learning processes for new members are best supported by experienced practitioners, particularly those who also understand the pressures and demands of headship. Whilst incumbent members of the organization and system are an undoubted source of support in this learning, it must be remembered that they are already part of those social processes and one of the key decisions of your headship will be whether you want to go with the flow or make changes to your school. Making sense of this often requires an external perspective and colleagues in similar positions, but in different school systems, are often best placed to give you impartial advice and counsel.

Role Adoption

The need for a different perspective can be also seen, for example, in the socialization process operated by a school community. When following on from a strong role model, the social pressure (sociality) requires a new member to become part of a serial socialization process; where no significant role model exists that new member may build a whole new role. The school community may, for example, be seeking to continue a pattern of success and would be anxious to appoint a headteacher who would continue in much the same manner as their predecessor. This would be a *serial* appointment, seeking similar attributes and behaviour from the incoming headteacher, whereas a school community seeking change would be making a *disjunctive* appointment as it sought to break with the behaviours of a previous incumbent. It would not be unusual, for example, to find a school where either the funding agency or the governing body sought change, whilst the remainder of the school community expected more of the same or vice versa. Finding the intent and then achieving the appropriate balance would be the key skills of a newly appointed headteacher, a situation compounded by the fact that they bring their own perspective, aspirations and intent to the job.

Most people setting their sights on a headship have a sense of their ideal and the early days of incumbency can be characterized by the possible erosion of this same idealism. This is identified, in discussions about the stages of headship arising from various studies of the job, as a period of reconciliation when that idealism is either sustained or adapted to meet needs and circumstances, something that is discussed in more detail in Chapter 6.

Social pressures may also require that a new member divests themselves of old identities and concepts of self (*divestiture*) or must reaffirm and reinforce the existing self-concept (*investiture*). When a new occupation offers little challenge to their skills and values their existing sense of self, a new member is reinforced and affirmed. When the demands of a new position are such that there is a need to make substantial adjustments to a new member's self-concept and their professional identity is challenged, divestiture occurs. It is interesting to hear the views of serving headteachers in this regard, when they talk of losing a sense of identity, of being treated and judged differently both by colleagues and the wider school community (Daresh and Male, 2000). Research into Scottish schools also shows how incoming headteachers experience the need to relinquish some previous practices, even when these had been successful in previous work situations, and thus establish new practices in new jobs. These detachments and attachments were weighted as gains or losses accordingly (Draper and McMichael, 1998). More information on the gains and losses associated with detaching from a previous job and attaching to a new one can be found in Chapter 6.

Moving into Role

Adapting these aspects of the socialization process to the work situation immediately demonstrates the potential for a large range of responses from the organization itself and from attendant organizations in a social system. Headteachers are generally appointed to a school (the organization) to follow a previous incumbent who may have been a positive or negative role model and may have left for a multitude of reasons (promoted, sacked, retired, dead) and left behind an accompanying image and memory. Consequently they may be expected to do nothing, something or everything in terms of style, social interaction and leading change. New headteachers can also experience disjunctive socialization if they differ significantly from the characteristics of those commonly appointed to the position. Women appointed to the post of head of a secondary school, for example, or someone from an ethnic minority appointed to the position of headteacher may have to negotiate their way through any ambiguity with less help because there have been few similar role models and sources of support (Valverde, 1980; Shakeshaft, 1987; Ortiz and Marshall, 1988; Scheurich, 1995; Coleman, 1996).

The demands of a larger system also impact on the expectations of a new headteacher, with national and local government both contributing to the creation of an environment that determines both the means and the ends of a school process. Employers are usually keen to ensure that administrative routines are understood, with much in the way of their sponsorship for induction processes favouring those ends rather than the wider issues. Central government in England has made a significant impact on the school process in the last quarter of the twentieth century through a raft of legislation and the introduction of market genre, with a national system of inspection that has become the principal enforcement mechanism for government policies which, as has already been argued in Chapter 1, largely determined the management structure and process of maintained schools.

The existence of such a wide range of intervening variables makes it extremely difficult to predict the induction and development needs of a new headteacher. Some issues are personal and relate to the development of their self-concept and self-image in their quest for an occupational identity. Other issues are specific to the context of a school and are set largely within a local social system that does not lend itself to generalization in terms of determining a framework of preparation and support on a national scale. Finally, some of the agenda of national government may have stifled creativity at the local level, producing a custodial orientation whereby innovation is curtailed by the need to ensure minimum standards of performance (Jones, 1986). New headteachers therefore face issues of divestiture as they realign their previous experience and expertise with the demands of a new job, requiring them to have some personal support in preparation for, and through, the early stages of incumbency.

Adapting to the Demands of a New Job

The majority of headteachers have managed their own preparation and induction to the point where they have achieved their occupational identity and this is still the likelihood for the foreseeable future. Even with the introduction of formal licensure schemes, preparation and induction processes are insufficiently developed to provide appropriate support to headteachers as they enter schools. With the exception of the New Visions programme run by the NCSL, induction processes in England still fail to provide the opportunity for incoming headteachers to explore the personal, organizational and systemic challenges within non-judgemental and/or mutually supportive environments. Research into this aspect of headship demonstrates the centrality of such relationships in establishing effective support systems.

Consequently learning to be the new formal leader of an organization has been 'dependent on the mix of people, issues, power and events that happen to coincide' (Weaver-Hart, 1993) rather than being an understood and planned process. Preparation and induction need not be hostages to fortune, however, as we know the key elements of the transition process.

Creating Decision-space

The single key factor that determines the success of transition to headship is the willingness of the newcomer to adapt to their new circumstances in the quest to meet the needs of the school community they are to serve. This is best supported by a knowledge of theories for action that allow for the unexpected and unknown to be evaluated before decisions are made and for alternative solutions to challenges to be developed, rather than using pre-conceived responses to perceived situations.

This is the true art of formal leadership, to be able to create what I call 'decision-space'. This is the skill to examine and explore issues for what they are, rather than what we expect them to be. To be successful in this regard you have to be prepared to deal with uncertainty, a practice to which we have not been conditioned as Anglo cultures militate against this kind of introspection, instead expecting firm and speedy decision making from our leaders. This is a very personal issue and one that can cause a great deal of unrest and discomfort in the early part of accession to post.

The first aspects of the transition that typically emerge on the personal and organizational routes are surprise, isolation and loneliness. My research and that of others active in this field indicates that such feelings and conditions are best countered through discourse with others who understand the pressures and challenges of headship, followed by a growing capability to be reflective and, ultimately, to become emotionally intelligent.

Talking to others who understand your situation is usually referred to as 'mentoring'. This can operate at a number of levels, including at a personal level (in conjunction with a family member or close friend), at a collegial level (within the organization), with peers (other beginning headteachers) or with seasoned veterans (with or without the direct knowledge of your school). Mentoring is not to be confused with coaching, which is the act of teaching someone how to do something 'correctly', as the former is an interactive relationship which will allow you to examine issues and challenges in the search for possible solutions.

My favourite definition of mentoring is provided in the evaluation of the Headteacher Mentoring Scheme (Bolam et al., 1993). They describe 'mentoring' as a generic term, covering a variety of activities, all aimed at providing support for new entrants to a job. The list of such activities includes advising, counselling, coaching and training, with the processes to be both 'non-evaluative and non-prescriptive'. In this definition the onus is on postholders to resolve their own problems and issues within their organizational context, thus providing the opportunity to be specifically focused rather than contingent on a set of generic competences. The advice and counselling received through a mentoring relationship thus provide support for the issues arising from the personal and organizational route to effective headship, whilst coaching and training are issues for the occupational route.

Mentoring was identified as the major support mechanism by respondents to my national survey, with nearly half (643 serving headteachers) identifying this in an open question as the most effective mode of support during the first year of a new headship and even more identifying the process as being just as important throughout the second year. It is vital to note that mentoring does not need to be supplied by just one person and, although you may choose an official mentor or have one appointed to you, you are likely to turn to a number of sources in order to make sense of your new reality. We will look at some possible mentoring models in more depth in Chapter 6, but suffice it for now to say that mentoring is clearly the single most effective mode of support as you move through the early stages of the personal and organizational route of a new headship.

Ultimately you should be aiming for self-sufficiency in terms of resolving challenges and issues and this is where reflection and emotional intelligence are desired behaviours. Reflection is the art of thinking through issues and developing possible solutions. There are two aspects to reflection: *reflection-on-action* and *reflection-in-action*. Most of us engage in reflection-on-action where we go over previous events in our mind or explore possible solutions to pending issues, but all the time in those moments away from the cause of our thoughts. These can be deliberate thinking sessions or an invasive version, which causes you to daydream or, worse still, to lie awake at night. Reflection-on-action is a considered process, therefore, even when it does interfere with your concentration or beauty sleep.

Reflection-in-action is a much more dynamic and immediate process, however, where possible solutions are played out against certain criteria during the course of the actual incident. Confronted, say by an angry parent, you need to think on your feet and check possible responses against your preferred code of conduct and the values you hold in relation to the behaviour you are witnessing. Most headteachers I know, for example, would not respond to aggression with aggression as they hold values that correspond to civilized behaviour. They would be seeking to do two things – to defuse the tension in the situation (thus buying time for decision space) and to evaluate their likely responses so as not to compromise their principles.

Emotional Intelligence

This brings me to the notion of Emotional Intelligence (EI). EI became very popular around the beginning of the new millennium and was touted frequently as a leadership quality of major proportions. Unfortunately EI is one of those two word buzz-phrases that have become popular in educational jargon that mean everything whilst telling us very little. In other words the concept is all-embracing, yet we do not have clear guidelines as to how to get or develop it. Generally all we know is that effective leaders have a high Emotional Quotient (EQ) and are intelligent in the use of emotions. EI corresponds very well to two of Gardner's models of multiple intelligences – intrapersonal and interpersonal intelligence (Gardner, 1997). People who know themselves very well have a high level of intrapersonal intelligence, whilst people who understand the motives and actions of others are deemed to have high levels of interpersonal intelligence.

EI can be represented as a continuum, however, that draws upon the individual ability to understand and react appropriately to any given social situation. Some people do this intuitively, whilst others prefer to engage in systematic analysis, with these two aspects representing the polar extremes of the EI continuum. Central to the continuum is the practice of reflection which, in turn, displays two dimensions of reflection-on-action and reflection-in-action. The continuum I have described is represented in Figure 2.2.

	On action		In action	
Systematic Enquiry	↔	**Reflection**	↔	**Intuition**

Figure 2.2 The Emotional Intelligence Continuum
© Trevor Male

The key to this model is to understand the process of reflection. As I have shown above, reflection-on-action is an after-the-event activity, when the intensity of the original event has receded, whilst reflection-in-action describes the capability to make judgements and decisions during the course of the event. In order to undertake reflection-in-action in an effective manner, the individual must have a set of core values and beliefs that allows them to compare and contrast the possible effectiveness of various actions whilst still engaged in the original event. Hopefully you can now see why intuition, a seemingly unconscious process, is at one end of the continuum and systematic enquiry is at the other end. Intuition is an instinctive process which can generally be deconstructed at a later stage by reflecting on action and invariably displays adherence to a set of values and beliefs which, in this instance, are applied at a sub-conscious level in much the same way as some grooved physical activities can be undertaken.

The problem with EI comes when the continuum is offered as a hierarchy of leadership behaviour, with intuition and reflection-in-action deemed to be higher order activities. Where this occurs it is a reflection of society rather than an indictment of the individual. Western societies, as I have shown, generally favour instinctive decision making in their leaders and reify those who can make decisions quickly, particularly if these lead to effective action. An effective leader, however, is one who makes effective decisions and who can often create the necessary 'decision-space' in order to consider a range of actions. An ineffective leader is the one who makes a decision in haste and then attempts to justify the action even when the outcome can be shown to be of limited use. There is no need, therefore, for individuals to chastise themselves if they engage in systematic enquiry or reflection-on-action as their preferred mode of leadership action. They are still working along the EI continuum, reconciling their values and beliefs with others in the pursuit of effective decision making.

Effective Theories for Action

The ability to create decision-space is contingent on your willingness to engage with the unknown and to do this effectively you may have to review your theories for action. A wide-ranging investigation into the formulation of effective theories for action as regards increasing professional effectiveness (undertaken over thirty years ago) is still relevant in this regard. The enquiry showed that individuals prefer to establish and sustain a number of governing variables that allow them to create a degree of constancy in their environment (Argyris and Schön, 1974). Various strategies are then employed to keep the value of those variables within an acceptable range which frequently, they conclude, results in what is termed 'Model I' behaviour. Model I behaviours are posited on individual design and management of the environment, with self-protection as a key motive. In establishing and maintaining such an environment, the individual engages in a number of activities that are manifested as defensive and political behaviours with a consequent restriction on innovation and creativity (Argyris and Schön, 1974). If the individual is the lead person in that environment then the organizational effectiveness is similarly affected.

Headship is characterized, however, by conflict and challenge, much of which emanates from other individuals in the social system who may resist being controlled and seek to influence decision-making processes. As discussed in the previous chapter, the willingness of colleagues in Anglo societies to submit to individual authority becomes less as their own status and standing grow. The consequence for headteachers is that they will have a reduced capability to control the range of governing variables and may find their own values questioned in their new role, whereas in previous experience they were more capable of sustaining those values and variables (Argyris and Schön, 1974). Their response should be to adopt 'Model II' behaviours, whereby they seek to design environments where other participants can develop responses to the various challenges faced by the organization and can gain experience of making things happen. In such organizations tasks are controlled jointly and protection of the individual and each other becomes a joint enterprise, with the organization and the individuals within it oriented toward growth.

The attractiveness of Model II is its acceptance of a non-linear environment. Its application to headship is relevant given an understanding of organizational dynamics, but it becomes even more relevant when considering the extent and rate of change that has become a feature of school systems. Occupational competence as a headteacher in this context requires the development of an individual theory of practice, consisting of the combination of practical technique and interpersonal capability. Headteachers, should thus be exemplars of Model II behaviours, a challenge that may prove difficult if previous experience (and success) were posited on Model I behaviours.

Assuming the argument for Model II behaviours to be acceptable, even desirable, for formal school leadership, help and guidance for making the transition are deemed variable according to personal circumstances, but are usually based on the principles of effective professional learning which:

1 is based on personally caused experience;
2 is usually produced by expressing and examining dilemmas;
3 values individuality and expression of conflicts;
4 must be guided by an instructor who has more faith in the participants than they have in themselves; who recognizes the limits of participants' learning methodologies; whose idea of rationality integrates feelings and ideas, and; who can encourage spontaneity. (Argyris and Schön, 1974: 98).

In Conclusion

The transition to formal leadership will require you to travel along two routes – the occupational and the personal/organizational – with each presenting different, but complementary, challenges. The resolution of personal and organizational challenges, typically exposed during the first year of tenure, should allow you to reconcile your skills and talents with the demands of the new job. This may mean you need to divest previous behaviours and develop new skills as you seek to manage this transition. Discussion in this chapter demonstrates that you will need to build upon your previous learning, gained through occupationally focused development and/or life experiences, in order to make sense of your new environment. The best support for that growth is, firstly, to recognize the need to think differently as formal leader and to remain open to a range of choices in the resolution of challenges and opportunities that will emerge now you are in charge. Subsequently you will need to develop your capacity to be reflective in your quest to become emotionally intelligent. When those attributes become part of your normal mode of operation you have reached the launch pad of effectiveness as the formal leader. At that point you can become strategic and begin to build the type of leadership capacity in others that supports high performance. You will, in short, have reached the high plains of leadership.

To adapt and learn from these messages from formal leadership, in general headteachers will need to develop support systems that will allow them to make the transition from licensed to effective practitioner. In the absence of systemic forces to assist this transition – sadly still the case more often than not – this process will require a good deal of self-management involving mentoring and peer support. The tools and learning experience needed for this programme of self-managed development are to be found in Chapter 6, but for now simply recognize that there is no automatic rescue system for struggling headteachers and that you are the most important person in defining the support you will need to make a successful transition to headship.

3 | Preparing for headship

The Decision

From the first moment you decided to apply for headship you began the process of conscious preparation for the job. Before that you had probably accumulated a number of personal and job experiences that prepared you for headship, but had not thought of yourself as a headteacher, so were moving toward the job in an unconscious mode. Some applicants to headship will have made the decision early in their life or in their career that some day they would like to be a headteacher. Others will make this later, and probably after some years of teaching experience, choosing to go for headship as they realize they are capable and willing.

There is a third category of prospective headteacher, however; those who had not thought of applying for headship until circumstances revealed them not only to be a viable candidate, but possibly the only one equipped to take on the job. The last of these categories typically includes seasoned teachers from small schools who find there is no real alternative and are persuaded, sometimes against their judgement, to take on the mantle of headship.

Headship in the Twenty-first Century

For most of the twentieth century headship positions were filled by willing applicants, who were mainly successful in the job. Annual reports from the Chief Inspector of Schools in England demonstrate significant levels of improvement in headteacher capability over the years to the point where it is now rare to find examples of incompetence or poor performance. Indeed by 2005 he has deemed that leadership and management are good or better in the majority of nursery and primary schools and unsatisfactory in only one in 20. Meanwhile he adjudged leadership and management to be good or better in three-quarters of secondary schools. Interestingly, however, he signalled that leadership was generally considered to be better than management, a factor most commonly seen in special schools (Office for Standards in Education, 2005). The Ofsted findings thus reinforce once more the need for headship to be a combination of leadership, management and administration.

The reasons for this continued improvement are many, with the various influences being interconnected and interdependent, something I will explore in more detail later in this chapter. But at the beginning of the twenty-first century we have a problem of headteacher recruitment, with many posts remaining vacant due to a shortage of capable and willing applicants (Howson, 2005). It seems we can no longer rely on willing volunteers or press-ganged, seasoned veterans to sustain the supply of headteachers in England.

Systemically there is no clear solution to this problem and we appear to be grappling with two key issues as to the future of headship. On the one hand we have the desire to ensure that those appointed to the job have the capabilities and qualities to be successful once they are in post. This requirement has led to a heightened interest in the licensure of formal school leaders, with that process requiring completion of training and development activities that ensure applicants satisfy the criteria established for the licence to be issued. On the other hand we have insufficient intrinsic interest in the job to generate sufficient applicants to fill the number of posts we have in the system.

It is too early to say what solutions there are for this problem, although there is some evidence emerging that one way through this issue may be to reduce the number of posts by reorganizing the school system. In England, for example, there is government interest in removing surplus school places by closing, amalgamating or federating schools, which would consequently reduce the number of headships – thus solving the problem? This is an interesting thought, and one which I have a number of reservations about, although this is not the place to conduct such a discussion as what we should be interested in is how we can best support all types of aspirant headteachers.

Anticipatory Socialization

The whole period of preparation for headship was explained in the previous chapter as the process of anticipatory socialization, whether unconscious or conscious. Aspirant headteachers emerge from previous life experiences, engage in a number of pre-service and induction activities and become effective once they come to terms with the job. We already know that very few aspects of their preparation equip new headteachers to make the transition to effectiveness immediately on completion of their pre-service training and development, which means that adequate support systems must be in place for those new to the job, particularly first time appointments.

One of my favourite analogies for headship is that of driving a car. Before you can get your licence to drive you have to learn how to, a process in the

United Kingdom that requires you to learn the relevant parts of the law, to practise driving in the company of a licensed driver, and to pass a test where you are expected to display a range of approved driving skills. Once you have your licence you can then learn how to really drive, a process that requires different approaches and skills than those that allowed you to pass the test. As one primary school headteacher described it "Headship is like driving a car – you learn when you get on the motorway if you can drive or not – but sometimes that is too late!"

The analogy of driving holds good for second or subsequent headships as well. Once we know how to drive we tend to stick pretty much to the same routes and routines each day, so driving becomes a more relaxing and sometimes reflexive activity. Many are the times I have traversed part of my normal routes on a kind of mental 'autopilot' whilst my conscious thinking processes wrestle with other issues. Put me in a different traffic system, city or route, however, and not only am I on full alert, I am also less competent. In a strange city, for example, I am not sure where to position my car, which lane to use or where exactly my turn is. In consequence I drive slower or with less effect. The first response typically results in local drivers looming ever larger in my rear view mirror or steering me to places I did not want to go. If I choose not to slow down, however, I frequently go whizzing past my turn or fail to see it at all.

Second or subsequent headships present challenges in much the same way that driving in a different city or country tests your adaptive skills. You are experienced and can drive perfectly well, but you just don't know which is the correct lane to use or exactly which one is your exit lane at various junctions. It does not take you long to find out, but in the early stages of this transition you can find driving to be more taxing and stressful than it would be in your normal world.

Making the transition from novice to effective driver has three stages – learning in a protected environment, passing the test and, finally, making the changes necessary to your driving style in order to survive in the real world. The same stages can be applied on the way to becoming an effective headteacher. In this chapter we are investigating what you need to do to prepare for your test; in the two chapters that follow I will take you through what you need to do to pass and how you can then learn how to be a headteacher in action rather than one in aspiration.

One word of warning here is that the processes are not distinctly separate and much can be done in the preparation stage to contribute to the transition stage when you enter headship. Not all of those learning experiences are required to get your licence, however, so you need to keep an eye on the main challenge of headship, which is choosing the best combination of your knowledge, skills, attributes and qualities to become effective in the school to which you are appointed.

Appropriate Learning Experiences

Even with the advent of formal preparation and licensure schemes, such as the NPQH, most headteachers and principals still manage their own preparation and induction to the point where they achieve occupational identity. There are many reasons to suppose that they will need to continue to do so in the future and any time spent on preparing yourself for the ultimate demands of headship before accepting the post will be time well spent.

Very early work in the USA in the field of moving into the role of institutional leader demonstrated such people as needing a combination of formal education, apprenticeship and learning by doing (Lortie, 1975). These ideas were later developed to take account of the differing demands on institutional leaders in both the preparation phase and in the early stages of their new career, developing a tri-dimensional conceptualization of professional development for school leaders (Daresh, 1988). Conclusions from that study advanced the argument that people must receive preparation and support for their leadership roles by equal attention being paid to strong academic preparation, realistic guided practice in the field and the formulation of personal and professional capabilities to cope with the ambiguities associated with the responsibilities of school leadership.

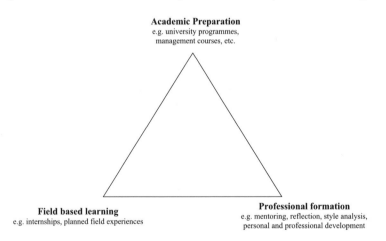

Figure 3.1 The tri-dimensional conceptualization of professional development for school leaders
Source: Daresh (1988)

The tri-dimensional model was then applied to the three commonly defined phases of school leadership – pre-service, induction and in-service – to demonstrate an appropriate balance of activity for each phase of professional development. The relative strengths of education, field-based learning and personal and professional formation differ as a person moves from pre-service through to induction and then on to the in-service phase.

All of the elements of the tri-dimensional conceptualization may be included in all three phases, with differing needs at different stages. As people move through career phases, however, learning is likely to occur more frequently from an experiential base. But there is never a point when either formal or field-based learning disappears entirely. The balance of each element at each phase is portrayed in Figure 3.2.

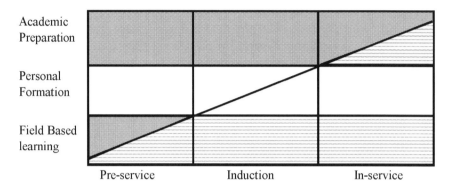

Figure 3.2 The tri-dimensional model of professional development and career development

Source: Daresh (1988)

This work on the professional development needs of school leaders is useful in suggesting the creation of an appropriate knowledge base through formal and informal learning experiences, coupled with an awareness that support for the continuing formation of personal and occupational identity is balanced appropriately through periods of pre-service, induction and in-service. The strength of the tri-dimensional model is the recognition that the dimension that tends to remain constant throughout all phases of a person's career is personal and occupational formation, that brings with it the need to engage in reflection, to think about one's personal ethical stances and one's commitment to the occupation.

Whilst this aspect of personal and occupational identity formation is considered constant, it is recognized that the issues to be considered will each differ at the individual level. Whilst we will explore this aspect more fully in the section on beliefs, values and principles to be found later in this chapter, the essential thing that needs to be recognized at this point is that individual beliefs and value systems will be challenged as you move into formal leadership positions and these may be subject to change. It is the intensity of the learning experiences you face as you prepare for and enter headship that determines at which point your ideals are compromised or changed. The greater the challenge the more assured you will be that the beliefs and values you hold are secure as you enter and manage the transition to effective headship.

Apprenticeship and Internship

The tri-dimensional model is not entirely appropriate for application to headship, however, as the nature of principal preparation in the USA is heavily dependent on university-led programmes in the pre-service stage. The emphasis in such programmes is generally on higher degree programmes with supplemental field-based learning experiences, such as a period of internship, required for those seeking certification as a principal. The model is thus informative rather than definitive in relation to the headship, but does provide us with important clues for those preparing for headship.

The formation of an appropriate knowledge base in pre-service in England traditionally has been largely field-based and informal, although national standards for headteachers have sought to formalize the curriculum and to remove the element of chance that was a feature of headship preparation in the last century. There is clear evidence to support the notion that this learning has enhanced the skill level of NPQH participants (Male, 2001) although the process has not and inherently cannot address the field-based learning needs of beginning headteachers in its present form. This is because the twin elements of apprenticeship and internship, key elements of the tri-dimensional model of professional development, are not integral to this particular licensure scheme.

My research also shows that the opportunities for gaining adequate in-school experience of leadership and management tasks and of working in an apprentice mode are still subject to chance and, in the case of primary schools, almost non-existent. The notion of apprenticeship is one of learning an art or trade through practical experience under skilled workers. Learning about headship in England had traditionally been a non-directed, incidental, in-school experience, although that changed following the introduction of the NPQH.

Today the personal evaluation and validation of in-school learning experiences are an integral part of the formal preparation for headship. This learning often requires structuring as few schools have a planned set of experiences designed to ensure leadership development. Obviously there have been many headteachers who have encouraged the rounded development of their senior staff to the point where they are prepared for headship, but the expediency of school life and pressure on resources have more frequently militated against such provision. It is rare, for example, to find a deputy headteacher in a primary school in England who does not also have a large teaching commitment. Finding time to engage in a range of challenging activities has not been a regular feature of life in primary schools and deputy headteacher responsibilities have tended to focus on management rather than leadership activities (Shipton and Male, 1998). Aspirant headteachers in special schools, meanwhile, report fewer opportunities to engage in middle management, remaining classroom practitioners for longer than their counterparts in other types of schools (Male and Male, 2001).

Greater opportunities for personal development as a prospective head-teacher typically occur in secondary schools where the larger numbers of pupils and adults employed require more strata within institutions. Even so, it is possible for people to have limited experiences that allow them to develop as the school leaders of the future. When assessing applications for the early stages of the NPQH, for example, it was common to find candidates engaged in a range of activities, but having direct responsibility for few of these. A key factor in managing your learning for future accreditation, therefore, is to ensure you can identify the impact you have had in terms of your leadership and management behaviour and activity.

Field-based Learning

There is still a need to provide structure and planning to field-based learning experiences, therefore, and this has been one of the strengths of a licensure programme such as the NPQH. Participants have to demonstrate their engagement in a range of activities and evaluate their contribution to leadership processes within school, with particular regard to the resolution of issues relating to school improvement. That self-evaluation is conducted against published criteria for the licensure scheme, such as the national standards for headteachers, and validated by an internal and external agent. The serving headteacher of an NPQH candidate will normally be the internal validator, whilst the external validation will be conducted by an NCSL consultant.

Licensure schemes such as the NPQH can thus claim to provide a degree of rigour to the pre-service stage of headteacher development. Such schemes would benefit from a further dimension to such learning, however, to one where the aspirant school leader is required to engage in leadership activities beyond their existing environment. Principal preparation programmes in the USA typically require a period of internship as a pre-requisite to licensure. The definition of 'intern' used here is a graduate who is receiving practical training in the workplace. The essential ingredient that distinguishes an intern from an apprentice is that internship will take place in an environment that is different from their normal workplace. Theoretically the challenge of working in a different environment will mirror many of the features of early headship, such as the need to develop new relationships with unfamiliar people and to effect change in a context where you have less than full knowledge of local circumstances and organizational culture.

In truth the experience of internships in the USA has been variable, favouring a model of learning depending more upon theory than the practical reality of placement. Yet there has been no real history of internship in England, with formal preparation heavily dependent on internal apprentice models of learning. Whilst the NPQH does require candidates to engage with and visit other schools, there is no expectation of direct involvement in leadership and management activities within those schools. Furthermore the type of school they are typically expected to visit is one with proven success, which may not be of direct relevance to their preferred or aspirational appointment as a headteacher. This absence of an internship requirement is unfortunate for two reasons. Firstly, and as described above, there is a greater chance that such an experience will bring with it challenges that reflect the transition to headship more accurately than those that may be found in the existing school. Secondly, the experience will expose the aspirant headteacher to leadership and management practice that may be qualitatively different than that within their existing school. This, of itself, may be helpful in determining future styles of headship.

Although it was suggested in Chapter 2 that most people model their behaviour as headteacher on role types they had previously experienced, especially during the early days of headship, there are some interesting counter findings from research that suggest some headteachers actually create their individual style in antithesis to previous experience (Ribbins, 1997; Weindling and Pocklington, 1996). In other words, they seek to be different from their previous headteachers as they see shortcomings they do not want to replicate: perhaps another good reason for looking at other role models.

The message for aspirant headteachers, therefore, is to seek to broaden your experience before applying for headship and to be aware of and learn from experiences beyond your own school. That message exhibits strong characteristics towards the principles of effective professional learning that recognize the need for a theory base consolidated through action (Argyris and Schön, 1974). Field-based learning is, in effect, simulation; a learning situation where you can try things without being ultimately responsible for the consequences of your actions.

As I described earlier, you can delegate responsibility but not accountability, so serving headteachers who encourage you to engage in active learning situations are thus taking a risk and, presumably, evaluating the consequences of that risk before letting you loose. Such opportunities remain as simulation, however, which is recognized as a higher order activity in adult learning, resulting in some transfer of skill as well as knowledge (Joyce and Showers, 1988), but apprentice and internship models that deliberately take aspirant headteachers into challenging situations have not been a part of any formal preparation programme in England and have seldom featured in individual preparation processes. Learning to be a headteacher has rather been self-managed and open to chance. It also appears to have been posited largely on unconscious learning experiences, some as a result of life histories as well as during the period of work-related anticipatory socialization.

To be an effective headteacher you really need to plan for appropriate learning experiences, as many of the things you could be involved in as a serving headteacher could be replicated or experimented with during the pre-service era as simulated activities. Such proactive behaviour will take you beyond the requirements for your 'licence', but will almost certainly set you up more completely for the demands of headship.

Knowledge and Personal Qualities

The search for a comprehensive knowledge base for headship continues. One hundred years plus of effort in the field in the USA, for example, and attempts to codify the knowledge base of educational administration continue to be contended mainly on the basis that there were no consistent features of organizations that allowed for the generation of universal laws (Culbertson, 1988). Furthermore, it was argued, once attempts are made to legitimate certain knowledge the interests of some individuals and groups are served, whilst the interests and concerns of other groups are thwarted. In identifying and legitimizing knowledge we are, in essence, engaging in a political act (Donmoyer et al., 1995). The search for a comprehensive knowledge base will thus remain complicated whilst political forces continue to promote an ideal model of headship rather than recognize the unique nature of each headship and there is a need for active debate on this issue at a time when some theorists and government agencies are more inclined to offer answers rather than to ask questions.

Appropriate Knowledge

Greater efforts have been made in the USA to identify an apolitical knowledge base than in the UK where aspirational models have been devised, often in concert with government ambitions. There is no clear evidential base used, for example, in the selection of the knowledge, personal qualities and actions expected for headteachers contained in the national standards for headteachers, as I will argue more extensively in the next chapter. In the USA, however, there has been a concerted effort to devise an appropriate body of knowledge for school leaders in relation to certain parameters. Seven general categories of knowledge were devised in the last years of the twentieth century by a consortium of ten key, national, school administration-related organizations to frame the discussion (National Policy Board for Educational Administration, 1989). The seven categories were:

- societal and cultural influences on schooling;
- teaching and learning processes and school improvement;
- organizational theory;

- methodologies of organizational studies and policy analysis;
- leadership and management processes and functions;
- policy studies and politics of education;
- moral and ethical dimensions of schooling.

From this starting point, following subsequent widespread discourse and further consortium work, a set of standards for licensure of school principals was devised and published by the Interstate School Leaders Licensure Consortium (ISLLC) in 1996, with the standards subsequently adopted by some 35 states (Weindling, 2003).

The ISLLC's standards cover six areas of knowledge; and coincidentally, so do the national standards for headteachers in England. Comparing the two sets shows a commonality of knowledge areas, with the single exception of ISLLC Standard 5 which refers to the moral and ethical issues relating to school leadership (see Table 3.1). The importance of professional accountability shines here, whilst the emphasis within the national standards for England is on external accountability. The major difference between the two sets of standards, however, can be seen in the language employed. The US version is open to interpretation and application whereas the English version is almost directive in nature. This demonstrates the aspirational nature of the English system, rather than the process of determining a generic knowledge base.

The outcome of this debate is that there is no simple answer as to the knowledge and personal qualities you will need as a headteacher as we have yet to address all the possible permutations. The fundamental issue in this regard is that the purpose of schooling is still not apparent in England, with no declaration of intent or human right underwriting a law that requires the compulsory education of children. The only definition we have is one that requires children between the ages of five and sixteen years of age to be educated full-time in accordance with their age and ability. The principal consequences of this undefined purpose are variable patterns of provision and measures of success. There is no requirement for any child of compulsory school age to attend school, for example, providing they are receiving an 'adequate education' (even though we still do not have clarity over this definition).

As a direct result there is about 1 per cent of all children in England being educated 'otherwise', usually in home education, with this number continuing to grow. A further 7 per cent of all children are in private schools, which are not subject to the same legal requirements as maintained schools and can thus determine their own provision. Both these types of provision are still subject to inspection and approval by Ofsted, however, in a similar way to all other types of educational provision for children of compulsory school age. The majority of children thus attend maintained schools, but even then there is considerable variation between local school systems across the country.

Table 3.1 Comparison of Standards for Principals (USA) and Headteachers (England)

ISLCC Standards	National Standards for Headteachers
1 By facilitating the development, articulation, implementation, and stewardship of a vision of learning that is shared and supported by the school community.	**Creating the future:** Critical to the role of headship is working with the governing body and others to create a shared, strategic vision and plan which inspire and motivate pupils, staff and all other members of the school community. This vision should encapsulate the headteacher's educational values and moral purpose whilst being inclusive of stakeholders' values and beliefs. The strategic planning process is critical to sustaining school improvement and ensuring that the school moves forward for the benefit of its pupils.
2 By advocating, nurturing, and sustaining a school culture and instructional programme conducive to student learning and staff professional growth.	**Leading Learning and Teaching:** Providing effective learning and teaching is a core principle of headship. Headteachers therefore have a central responsibility for the quality of learning and teaching and for pupils' achievement. This implies setting high expectations and monitoring and evaluating the effectiveness of learning outcomes. The learning culture thus created should enable pupils to become effective, enthusiastic, independent learners, committed to life-long learning.
3 By ensuring management of the organization, operations, and resources for a safe, efficient, and effective learning environment.	**Developing self and working with others:** Effective relationships are important in headship as headteachers work with and through others, including pupils, staff, governors, parents and other members of the community. Effective headteachers manage themselves and their relationships well. Headship is about building a professional learning community which enables others to achieve. Through performance management and effective continuous professional development, the headteacher supports all staff to achieve high standards. All headteachers should be committed to their own continuous professional development in order to equip themselves with the capacity to deal with the complexity of the role and the range of leadership skills and actions required of them.
4 By collaborating with families and community members, responding to diverse community interests and needs, and mobilizing community resources.	**Managing the organization:** Headteachers need to provide effective organization and management for the school they lead and seek ways of improving organizational structures and functions. Headteachers should ensure that the school and the people and resources within it are organized and managed to provide an efficient, effective and safe learning environment. These management responsibilities imply the re-examination of the roles and responsibilities of those adults employed to work in the school, capacity building across the workforce, managing available resources and ensuring value for money through effective performance management.
5 By acting with integrity, fairness, and in an ethical manner.	**Securing accountability:** With values at the heart of their leadership, headteachers have a professional responsibility to the whole school community. In carrying out this responsibility, headteachers are accountable to a wide range of groups, particularly pupils, parents, governors and the LEA. Additionally, headteachers are responsible for ensuring collective responsibility in order that all members of the school community accept they are accountable for the contribution they make to school outcomes. Headteachers are legally and contractually accountable to the governing body for the school, its environment and all its work.
6 By understanding, responding to, and influencing the larger political, social, economic, legal, and cultural context.	**Strengthening community through collaboration:** Schools exist in an individual social context, which has a direct impact on what happens inside the school. School leadership should commit to engaging with the internal and external school community, thus modelling the principles of equity and entitlement. Headteachers should encourage and engage in collaboration with other schools in order to bring positive benefits to their own organization and share its expertise more widely. Headteachers should ensure collaboration and collective responsibility for the wellbeing of children with parents and carers and across multiple agencies, at both strategic and operational levels.
	Headteachers should be aware that school and community improvement are interdependent and that they share responsibility for leadership of the

Adapted from ISLLC and National Headteacher Standards

Furthermore, at the time of writing we also now have several secondary schools being made independent, some federations of schools working to different statutes than other maintained schools and the prospect of every maintained school being turned into an independent trust with the attendant freedom to choose best practice. When you add an indeterminate factor called 'success' to this equation, the opportunity to identify any similarity between schools decreases significantly, as does the opportunity to identify the body of knowledge needed for headship.

Ultimately the 'answer' is specific to the school to which you are appointed and to the situations in which you find yourself. Having said that there are commonalities to be found between headships and these can be grouped together in terms of the personal and occupational dimensions identified in Chapter 2. In other words there are some features of headship that are common, whilst effective headship is about choosing the combination of actions that is appropriate to your school.

Skills and Personal Qualities

In the main those knowledge bases that have been developed for formal school leadership have tended to identify skills and personal qualities as the bedrocks of successful behaviours. Skills can be separated into those dealing with technical issues or those dealing with social (moral) issues. Personal qualities, meanwhile, are more to do with a disposition to engage successfully with the demands of the job. Knowledge and understanding of appropriate theory are clearly required, although this has been given second order status in England where more emphasis has been placed on field-based learning and practical know-how. It is also becoming obvious that headteachers need a variety of leadership and management styles and an ability to interpret the collective reality of a school instead of pursuing unrealistic aims.

Taken together these factors place incredible demands on individual and systemic approaches to the effective preparation of those destined for headship and in truth many of the capabilities necessary to be successful in the job can only be learnt when in post. This places a strong emphasis on supporting the newly appointed headteacher through the induction phase, something I will explore more fully in Chapter 6. Effective preparation can be undertaken, however, as has been argued earlier in this chapter, particularly if you actively seek appropriate learning experiences.

So do not be deluded by checklists of skills and personal qualities, for the development of an effective skills base does not seem to have been a major issue for the vast majority of headteachers. My research shows most headteachers perceiving themselves as well prepared or extremely well prepared for the range of personal and technical skills identified for the job (Male, 2004). I developed that particular checklist by using the outcomes of a study on the elements of successful principalship in the USA that employed the Delphi technique, a well-known research approach that seeks agreement between respondents to the point where there is no contention. By working closely with a number of willing volunteers in England I was able to adapt the list to match the demands of the job as perceived by serving headteachers. The subsequent survey results from over 1400 respondents demonstrated there to be few areas where people felt inadequately prepared in terms of the skills required for headship, with those who had completed the NPQH feeling even more capable. My investigation also demonstrated their development needs during the early stages of headship to be more focused on making sense of their new situation and coming to terms with the complex demands and decision making required by the job. There was no consistency in regard to training requirements for specific skills, with respondents indicating that they had usually managed to satisfy any such need through personally seeking appropriate training and coaching.

The key element of the new job was the rapid realization of its intensity. Responses from the survey showed this transition to be the metaphorical equivalent of walking into a beautiful garden only to step on a rake! The shock experienced on entry was typically expressed as an unanticipated factor in moving into headship. Central to such feelings was the sensation of not being in control, of not being able to nail things down as they had in the past. All of a sudden decision making was significantly more demanding as black and white issues turned greyer and greyer, hard edged concepts became slippery and the ground beneath their feet became less secure. Donald Schön describes this aspect of that land occupied by a new headteacher to be the same as swamp:

> In the varied topography of school practice, there is a high hard ground overlooking a swamp. On the high ground, manageable problems lend themselves to solution through the application of research-based theory and technique. In the swampy lowland, messy confusing problems defy technical solution. (Schön, 1987: 3)

The basic problem here is that individuals seek to establish a degree of constancy in their environment and then try to employ various strategies to sustain this environment. As argued in the previous chapter such behaviours are often defensive and political and can restrict innovation and creativity. Moving into headship means moving into uncertainty, however, and having to face the prospect of failure on a regular basis. Failure is inevitable as the demands of the job are not only insatiable, but all too frequently irreconcilable. This sensation is amplified when contrast is made with earlier career experiences which invariably have been characterized by success. The successful headteacher learns not to take these failures personally and works hard to limit the impact of any such failure. The effective headteacher learns new behaviours which allow for flexibility of response, a process already described in Chapter 2 as Model II behaviours (Argyris and Schön, 1974).

Model II behaviours require formal leaders to design environments where other participants can develop responses to the various challenges faced by the organization and can gain experience of making things happen. In such organizations tasks are controlled jointly and protection of both the individual and each other becomes a joint enterprise, with the organization and the individuals within it oriented toward growth. Its application to the role of a headteacher is relevant given an understanding of organizational dynamics, but it becomes even more relevant when considering the extent and rate of change that has been a feature of many schools. Occupational competence as a headteacher in this context requires the development of an individual theory of practice, consisting of a combination of practical technique and interpersonal capability – a unique response to a unique situation.

Personal Beliefs, Values and Principles

The outcome for headteachers of adopting Model II behaviours is that they may find their own values questioned in their new role, whereas in their previous experience they were more capable of sustaining those values and variables. Most respondents to my survey indicated they believed they had secure personal values on taking up their first headship and, certainly, aspirant headteachers in England are expected, by the time they qualify for the NPQH, to have identified core values and be able to conduct themselves in relation to those values. Effective headteachers will not only recognize the bases of those values, however, but will be able to continually explore and validate their value sets by accommodating challenge and making adaptations if necessary.

Values grow from beliefs and allow you to develop principles for action. The cycle begins with a set of beliefs about how we understand and deal with the world around us. From those beliefs you identify certain things of value which provide you with a basis for establishing principles to underpin any actions that follow. Values thus define standards of 'goodness, quality or excellence that undergird behaviour and decision-making' (Deal and Peterson, 1999).

In the case of school age education, for example, I believe the principal focus of attention should be towards the establishment, maintenance and continued development of environments that meet individual learning needs. I also hold dear that learning should be process rather than knowledge or skills based; in other words about helping individuals learn how to learn. From that belief I can identify my core values as children learning notions of equity, justice and respect which will help develop my preferred principles for action. My values thus correspond to the rights of children as learners in that they will be treated fairly and will be given every chance to retain their dignity, with these principles underwriting all subsequent actions. As formal leader I would seek to promote these values through my decision-making processes. I would, for example, look to ensure that decisions were based on the principle of ensuring the interests of children and their learning, ahead of the interest of adults within or outside the school community. I would seek to promote behaviour patterns that allowed for justice to prevail, support systems that provided children with equal chances of success and relationships that were based on mutual respect.

By their very nature, however, values are the consequence of subjective consciousness – they do not exist on their own and the world is devoid of notions of beauty, ugliness, right or wrong, good or bad, until we define those concepts. Once defined they become 'concepts of the desirable' (Hodgkinson, 1991: 89). To be successful in headship you must have a value set that corresponds to the social system in which you serve. We develop our beliefs and values through our experience and interaction with others and, in turn, can influence and shape the dominant value set in any community.

This process is governed by actions at five levels, where there is considerable potential for different values to overlap and to extend upwards and downwards. The first of these levels is self-interest, which is rarely achieved, however, as the influence and needs of the immediate group impact on pure self-interest. In personal life this would be the influence of family and friends; in the work situation it will be your immediate colleagues (Level 2). This informal grouping is further affected by the wants and needs of the organization (Level 3), nested within the immediate community (Level 4) and the ethos of society in general (Level 5), with desirable standards being affected at all these levels by the spirit of the times (the *Zeitgeist*). As a result some values are 'given', seemingly beyond dispute or contention, and these provide unspoken or unexamined assumptions.

In England, for example, two key agencies have stated their view as to the desirable values for the occupation of headteacher within the nation state, thus contributing to the establishment of a societal expectation at Level 5. The General Teaching Council (GTC) have issued a statement of professional values and practice for teachers (see Table 3.2) which they suggest should underpin behaviour and decision making within the teaching profession. Given that headteachers in maintained schools are normally qualified teachers, it seems reasonable to suppose the code applies equally to them.

The second agency to stake a claim for defining an appropriate value system is the Department for Education and Skills (DfES) which has issued a set of

Table 3.2 Professional Values and Practice for Teachers

Teachers seek to:	Through:
Inspire and lead young people	• helping them achieve their potential as fulfilled individuals and productive members of society; • having high expectations, helping all to progress regardless of personal circumstance, needs and backgrounds; • developing pupils intellectually and personally; • safeguarding pupils' general health, safety and well-being; • demonstrating the characteristics they are trying to inspire in pupils, including a spirit of intellectual enquiry, tolerance, honesty, fairness, patience, a genuine concern for other people and an appreciation of different backgrounds.
Work within a framework of legislation, statutory guidance and school policies with many lines of accountability and respond to a social situation that is continually changing	• attempting to achieve success for their pupils through a complex network of relationships; • challenging stereotypes and opposing prejudice in order to safeguard equality of opportunity; • respecting individuals regardless of gender, marital status, religion, colour, race, ethnicity, class, sexual orientation, disability and age.
Be competent classroom practitioners	• developing insight into the learning needs of young people; • applying professional judgement to meet those needs and choosing the best ways of motivating pupils to achieve success; • using assessment to inform and guide their work; • adapting their teaching appropriately to take account of new findings, ideas and technologies.
Work in collaboration with other adults	• supporting their colleagues in achieving the highest professional standards; • sharing their own expertise and insights in the interests of the people they teach; • being open to learning from the effective practice of their colleagues; • respecting the rights of other people to equal opportunities and to dignity at work; • respecting confidentiality where appropriate; • working in partnership with different professionals, the school governing body, support staff and other interested people within and beyond the school; • respecting the skills, expertise and contributions of these colleagues and partners and building productive working relationships with them in the interests of pupils.
Appreciate the importance of their own professional status in society	• demonstrating high levels of commitment, energy and enthusiasm; • responding sensitively to the differences in pupils' home backgrounds and circumstances and recognizing the importance of working in partnership with parents and carers to understand and support their children's learning; • using judgement over appropriate standards of personal behaviour; • taking responsibility for their own continuing professional development, through the opportunities available to them, to make sure that pupils receive the best and most relevant education; • continually reflecting on their own practice, improving their skills and deepening their knowledge.

Adapted from: *Statement of Professional Values and Practice for Teachers*, General Teaching Council (2005) expectations that underpin the national standards for headteachers which they have labelled as the Core Purpose of Headship (see Figure 3.3).

The Core Purpose of the Headteacher

The core purpose of the headteacher is to provide professional leadership and management for a school. This will promote a secure foundation from which to achieve high standards in all areas of the school's work. To gain this success a headteacher must establish high quality education by effectively managing teaching and learning and using personalised learning to realise the potential of all pupils. Headteachers must establish a culture that promotes excellence, equality and high expectations of all pupils.

The headteacher is the leading professional in the school. Accountable to the governing body, the headteacher provides vision, leadership and direction for the school and ensures that it is managed and organised to meet its aims and targets. The headteacher, working with others, is responsible for evaluating the school's performance to identify the priorities for continuous improvement and raising standards; ensuring equality of opportunity for all; developing policies and practices; ensuring that resources are efficiently and effectively used to achieve the school's aims and objectives and for the day-to-day management, organisation and administration of the school.

The headteacher, working with and through others, secures the commitment of the wider community to the school by developing and maintaining effective partnerships with, for example, schools, other services and agencies for children, the LEA, higher education institutions and employers. Through such partnerships and other activities, headteachers play a key role in contributing to the development of the education system as a whole and collaborate with others to raise standards locally.

Drawing on the support provided by members of the school community, the headteacher is responsible for creating a productive learning environment which is engaging and fulfilling for all pupils.

Source: Department for Education and Skills (2004)

Figure 3.3 The core purpose of the headteacher in England

The statements from the DfES and the GTC are both based on concepts of the desirable from a central perspective, however, rather than those established in empirically tested environments and provide implicit frames of reference for behaviour that have not been tested in practice. Consequently these should be considered as general points of reference rather than as a specific template for success and as advisory rather than statutory.

Close examination of the two documents reveals a political motive that needs to be examined in light of the needs of the school community you serve. Your school is not guaranteed success if you were to adopt these aspirations without qualification and, in some instances, you would be contravening the basic human rights and moral conventions for children if you were to follow slavishly the implicit guidance. Rather than act on such assumptions, therefore, the effective headteacher seeks to identify and enact the core values that are representative and appropriate to the school community they serve. Research conducted in England by the Hay McBer organization on 'breakthrough' leadership in schools demonstrates this principle in practice (Hay Group, 2002).

Breakthrough Leadership

The Hay Group are well known for large-scale studies into the characteristics of effective leaders and teachers and have been extensively commissioned for such research by the DfES. This particular study was very small, however, focusing on just ten headteachers who had done something dramatic or impressive in their schools, earning themselves the title of 'maverick headteacher' along the way. The report shows these headteachers as driven by a vision of their children's future, to have a ruthless streak and to not mind breaking the rules or going against the establishment to achieve goals for their students, whether academic or social. Underpinning their behaviour and school processes were values, established early in their headship, that sought the greatest good for the greatest number and were maintained through public reward and the punishment of transgressions. In pursuit of maintaining this value-driven culture they were prepared to question assumptions, take risks and make enemies, if necessary. The skills they deployed included connected thinking, building leadership capacity within the school and managing resources (financial, material and human) in support of student learning. The consequence is that they have delivered the 'right' results without using conventional methods. They are, the report concludes, pioneers in an age where the government message is for schools to take decisions that, within a framework of standards, are based on informed professional judgement.

It is important, therefore, that you seek to establish the value set that is meaningful to you and appropriate for your school community and to be prepared to constantly evaluate and review where necessary. It is a useful exercise to classify values as those that correspond to basic human rights, to general moral principles, to professional or occupational standards and to societal or political ends. Leithwood et al. (1994) have done just that when examining how to develop expert school leaders, identifying the basic human values as *survival, freedom, happiness, knowledge* and the *respect for others*, and general moral values as *carefulness, fairness* (or *justice*) and *courage*, none of which would be out of place in any civilized society. They then identify a range of professional and societal values relevant to the provinces of Canada where they conducted their research, many of which are important for other democratic western countries. The task is equally relevant to other countries, including England, and would represent time well spent in preparation for headship.

4 | National standards and the NPQH

Standards for School Leadership

The adoption of standards for school leaders is well on the way to becoming a global phenomenon with the introduction of standards for headteachers and principals in the USA, the UK, Australia and New Zealand, with other countries set to follow.

The use of standards to describe and evaluate headship has become central in England since their introduction to the national scene in 1997 as a precursor to the NPQH. There have been two further sets of standards published since then, with the latest version being published in 2004. The National Standards for Headteachers are based on three key principles and describe desired headteacher behaviour in six areas in an attempt by central government agencies to reflect the evolving role of headship in the early twenty-first century and to incorporate current government thinking and guidance (Department for Education and Skills, 2004). The purpose of the standards, in the view of the Department, is to:

> Recognize the key role that headteachers play in engaging in the development and delivery of government policy and in raising and maintaining levels of attainment in schools in order to meet the needs of every child. (DfES, 2004: 2)

The three key principles underpinning the standards are that the work of headteachers should:

- be learning-centred;
- be focused on leadership, and;
- reflect the highest possible professional standards.

The standards are designed to be generic and applicable to headteachers irrespective of phase and type of school. They are set out in six key non-hierarchical areas which when taken together, it is claimed, represent the role of the headteacher. These are:

- Shaping the Future
- Leading Learning and Teaching
- Developing Self and Working with Others
- Managing the Organization
- Securing Accountability
- Strengthening Community.

Within each of these the knowledge requirements, professional qualities (skills, dispositions and personal capabilities) and actions needed to achieve the core purpose are identified. This general statement is qualified in the published standards which suggest that whilst particular knowledge and professional qualities are assigned to one of the six key areas, they are interdependent and many are applicable to all key areas. Effective headteachers, they suggest, will be responsive to the context of their individual school in the choice of their actions and will maintain an overview of standards that integrates their work into a coherent whole.

The standards are intended by the DfES to have a range of uses in the recruitment of headteachers and in performance management processes. They have been devised in order to provide a framework for professional development and action and to supply guidance to all school stakeholders in what should be expected from the headteacher. The standards are central to the NPQH in that they determine the content of the preparation programme for aspirant headteachers and are then used to identify threshold levels of performance for the assessment framework.

So where did the standards come from and how important are they to you as a headteacher?

The Development of Standards

Pinning down the evolution of standards is not easy. Generally when you investigate the nature of a leadership and management tool you can pretty soon unravel a history of research and discussion that has informed its development. As described in the previous chapter you will find in the USA, for example, evidence of a search for the knowledge base of school administration stretching back over a century. In England, however, the first emergence of national standards for headteachers was shrouded in mystery as they transformed overnight from a contentious debate into a coherent set of standards that were immediately adopted for the new NPQH in early 1997.

Extensive and lively discussions amongst the pioneers of the NPQH about the focus for the new standards to be adopted was thus ended when the new standards were unveiled. I know this because I was one of those debating pioneers. Despite the many enquiries I have made since, however, I cannot ascertain who actually edited the ideas into the set of standards that were adopted. The standards have survived since their introduction in

1997, however, with all subsequent adaptations and amendments being incremental rather than fundamental. So do the standards provide an accurate picture of headship in action?

I made the contention in Chapter 2 that we do not have a theory base for headship and that we have appropriated our ideas about school leadership from other school systems and other theory bases. A similar argument can be mounted against the use of standards, in that it is not easy to identify their genesis and this is dangerous when we are so heavily reliant on them to judge the capability of our next generation of headteachers. Some clues for their centrality can be determined from the tradition of competence and competency that has its roots in the development of management theory in the USA during the 1960s.

Competence and Competencies

Many of the attempts to identify the characteristics of leadership have made use of job analysis in order to clarify the personal qualities, behaviours and traits needed to be effective. Early work on the identification of leadership and management potential was conducted by McLelland (1973) as part of a consultancy project commissioned by the American Management Association. The McBer Corporation built upon McLelland's work and conducted a major research exercise to determine the characteristics of managers who, it was claimed, were superior performers compared to the average (Boyzatis, 1982).

Assessment consists of two major approaches; the use of 'personal qualities', emanating mainly from the work of Boyzatis, or the use of an 'occupational standards' approach that details the standards required for the accreditation or evaluation of aspects of work roles. Attempts to explain the relationship between technical capability and the development of attitudes, values and beliefs appropriate for the job have sought to establish models of 'competence'. Once determined, models of 'competence' provide a template for training and development for and towards the relevant occupation.

The work undertaken by the McBer Corporation led to the development of the personal qualities approach, which became a critical component of effective management action and performance. In this model it was the combination of competencies exhibited by the individual, together with the demands of the job and the context of the organization, that determined effectiveness in action or performance. When all three components were aligned there was superior performance; where there was dissonance between the components there was average, limited or ineffective performance (see Figure 4.1).

The occupational standards approach to competence differs from the personal qualities approach in that it describes the outcomes that a leader, manager or management team has to achieve in order to demonstrate competent performance. This approach thus attempts to define benchmarks or specifications against which performance can be assessed. Both approaches start from a process of job analysis, but the personal qualities approach adopted by the McBer Corporation sees the identification of tasks/skills as an intermediate step in the identification of personal qualities. The McBer approach therefore describes the *personal components* that enable competency, while the occupational standards approach describes those *functions* of the job in which the person must be competent. The occupational standards approach, in general management terms, tends to define any characteristic that enhances a job holder's ability to perform effectively and thus divides into progressively smaller parts that have been used to detail the standards of work roles.

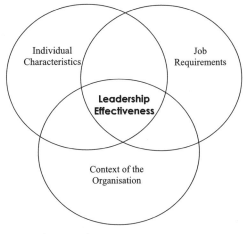

Figure 4.1 Management competency
Source: Boyzatsis (1992)

Spencer and Spencer (1983) attempted to draw the two approaches together through the metaphor of the iceberg. The behaviours, knowledge and skills are visible, 'above the water-line', and are thus observable. The traits, motives and abilities 'sit below the water-line' and contribute, in an invisible way, to skilled behaviour. In consequence there is a divergence in the description offered by each approach. The personal qualities approach describes those components of a person that enable him or her to be competent, while the occupational standards approach describes those functions of the job at which a person must be competent (Jirasinghe and Lyons, 1996).

Competence can thus be defined as the ability to undertake an aspect of a job effectively and efficiently and to consist of a number of competencies. A competent driver, for example, exhibits this competency in a number of actions when they undertake a certain manoeuvre, such as making a turn across oncoming traffic. The classic ritual of mirror–signal–manoeuvre demonstrates that the driver has checked traffic behind the vehicle and has indicated their intention before moving to the correct speed and road position to make the turn. They then consider the behaviour of oncoming traffic and, when content they have sufficient space and time to make the turn, move the car in an appropriate manner. Fundamental to all these actions is the physical capability to control the car. Competence, therefore, is the ability to make the turn whilst the range of competencies is both physical and mental. The incompetent driver is the one who either gets the sequence wrong or has an inadequate range of competencies to meet the physical and mental demands of making that turn across traffic. Competence is the overarching description of behaviour, therefore, and is contingent not only on the level of skill and knowledge but also on the ability to coordinate the various competencies in pursuit of the overall aim.

Headship and Models of Competence

Extensive claims have been made for a competence-based approach to developing headteacher capability and reflecting that into headship development and assessment processes. Discussion and theories of competence have been at the forefront of headteacher development in England since the early 1980s, with advocates of a competence-based approach claiming that it will provide a comprehensive and accurate picture of an 'education manager's job' and will contribute towards theory building and the creation of a framework for appraising performance (see for example Jirasinghe and Lyons, 1996). Programmes of preparation and support for headteachers, particularly since the early 1990s, are viewed as having been underwritten by notions of competence (Bush, 1998; Brundrett, 2001), with protestations from government agencies that this was not the case being dismissed as 'semantic nervousness' (Lumby, 1995: 11).

The National Education Assessment Centre (NEAC) was the first organization to employ the findings of a competence-based assessment process for headteachers in England, establishing a base in Oxford in 1992 from which they initially conducted the assessment process before franchising the work more widely. This was a charged service, originally set up by the Secondary Headteachers Association (SHA) in conjunction with the Oxford Polytechnic (later Oxford Brookes University), that applied the pioneering work of the National Association of Secondary School Principals (NASSP) in the USA who had been using the assessment centre approach for almost twenty years by the time the NEAC started their work (Jirasinghe and Lyons, 1996). Both the NASSP and the NEAC used 12 identified competencies which, they claimed, experience and research had shown as necessary for successful senior management in schools.

The approach adopted through the NASSP's and NEAC's standards was based more on the personal qualities model of competence than the development of occupational standards. Adaptation of this process of defining occupational standards for the job of headteachers had been undertaken around the same time, principally through the work of School Management South, a consortium of 14 LEAs funded by the government-sponsored School Management Task Force (SMTF) in the early 1990s. The consortium employed functional analysis to produce a set of occupational standards for school management for headteachers that contained 41 elements emanating from four key roles (Earley, 1992). This approach thus atomized the job of head-teacher and reduced it to lists of highly circumscribed task elements, skills or personal characteristics.

Headteacher Standards

Use of NEAC standards seemed to underwrite the list of tasks and abilities devised for the HEADLAMP scheme, launched in 1995, which is described as the first publication of 'headteacher competencies' (West-Burnham and O'Sullivan, 1998). The definition of a headteacher's role can be adjudged during the 1990s, however, as having proceeded more towards the occupational standards approach, as there were a number of efforts to establish task definition rather than the range of personal qualities needed to enact the role. The first set of national standards for headteachers tended to focus on the process of defining what Greenfield (1985) described as the 'technical' components of school leadership.

Central among the concerns of the Teacher Training Agency (TTA), the government agency responsible for shaping headteacher development in England from 1994 to 2000, was a guarantee of the suitability of a candidate for headship through the award of the National Professional Qualification for Headship or NPQH. Based on the National Standards for Headteachers, the NPQH was meant to signal that the holder had demonstrated their readiness for headship. It was not claimed, nor intended, to demonstrate that the holder was capable of fulfilling all aspects of the standards, but only that they were ready to take on the job.

Subsequently the standards have also been used as a template for performance for all headteachers and to define a number of other development programmes, including the Leadership Programme for Serving Headteachers (LPSH) first introduced by the TTA in 1998. The content of the LPSH programme is largely based on the competency clusters developed by the McBer Corporation, for which it is claimed that the 20 competencies in their original model cover 80 to 90 per cent of the distinguishing characteristics of superior performance in the jobs studied (West-Burnham and O'Sullivan, 1998). The trials period for the LPSH led to the development of a model of headship competency based on the McBer clusters. Interviews with some 65 serving headteachers, identified by Ofsted and the TTA as 'highly effective', resulted in the formulation of 15 characteristics for headteachers which came together 'to deliver highly effective performance in bringing about dramatic improvements and then sustaining them' (Teacher Training Agency, 1998: 21). These characteristics are grouped into five clusters to create 'models of excellence' (see Table 4.1).

Table 4.1   Characteristics of highly effective headteachers

Personal values and passionate conviction	Creating the vision
• Respect for others • Challenge and support • Personal conviction	• Strategic thinking • Drive for improvement
Planning for delivery, monitoring, evaluating and improving performance • Analytical thinking • Initiative • Transformational leadership • Teamworking • Understanding others • Developing potential	**Building commitment and support** • Impact and influence • Being and holding people accountable **Gathering information and gaining understanding** • Social awareness • Scanning the environment

Source: Teacher Training Agency (1998)

Work on the LPSH, conducted by a partnership consisting of the National Association of Headteachers (NAHT), the Hay McBer Corporation and the Open University, appears to be one of only two attempts to identify a range of competences that are specific to the occupation of headteacher, with an independent study conducted by Jirasinghe and Lyons (1996) laying claim to a similar process.

The conclusion that seems obvious from the history outlined above is that government-sponsored programmes of headship development are based on models of competence, although there is no recognition of the theory base in the publication of standards. The correlation is too strong to ignore, however, so how good are the standards at describing headship and developing effective headteachers?

The Problems with Standards

I can offer four aspects of concern over the National Standards. Firstly, the absence of a clear theoretical base raises questions about their ability to define the job. Secondly, they are aspirational in nature and contingent on a particular context. Thirdly, there is no gradation within the standards which leaves their application to be almost entirely subjective, particularly when judging the potential capability of an aspirant headteacher. Fourthly, they are posited on a model of individual leadership when we are now recognizing the centrality of mutual responsibility for school leadership.

These issues coalesce in practice. The examination I conducted above of the development of models of competence shows this to have been the most likely theoretical base for these standards and you can see evidence of the two approaches within the new standards which illustrate each key area with exemplars of knowledge, personal qualities and abilities. The key concern here, however, is that the two aspects of competence – the personal qualities or occupational standards approach – are in conflict when applied to the process of identifying and developing headteachers. The occupational standards approach is useful in assisting with the identification of the skills and attributes of aspirant headteachers, yet such an approach would do little to help with the application of these to different work or organizational settings. The personal qualities approach, however, would be more applicable to creating the flexibility and adaptability needed for headship in action.

Failure to distinguish between the two approaches can lead, therefore, to the subjective use of the standards when assessing the actual and potential qualities of a headteacher. Without any form of gradation the range of standards is open to interpretation, consequently giving rise to the possibility that the definition of a 'qualified' headteacher is a hostage to fortune. Unfortunately, perhaps, early attempts by the TTA to devise greater clarity by the use of exemplars of performance, such as defining the characteristics of an 'Expert Headteacher' (Teacher Training Agency, 1996) never really got off the drawing board.

There has been work within the LPSH programme, however, to draw together a range of competences that are evident in relation to different types or phases of schools. A four-point assessment strategy has been devised for each competency by Hay McBer and participants on the LPSH programme are graded accordingly (see Table 4.2). Analysis of the emerging data from the early stages of the programme allowed for the definition of clusters of competence levels that were associated with different types of schools (Dunphy and Scott, 2000). Effective headteachers of small primary schools (fewer than 200 pupils), for example, demonstrated three baseline competencies at an appropriate level, supplemented by a range of other competence clusters.

Overall, headteachers were expected to have at least six of the 15 competencies at Level 2 and the remaining nine at Level 3. Further work of this nature will be needed if the standards are going to be more useful in the future and to thus avoid the tag of being politically acceptable, but practically useless.

What should be evident from my previous discussion, however, is that effective headship is achieved when appropriate choices of behaviour are made by the formal school leader. Attempting to apply a universal, generic set of behaviours to formal school leadership denies the specific nature of the school to which the headteacher has been appointed. Effective headteachers exhibit a range of leadership, management and administrative skills that are appropriate to the circumstance to which they are either appointed or they themselves have created subsequently.

Table 4.2 Headteacher characteristics – small schools

Cluster 1	Cluster 2	Cluster 3	Cluster 4
Any two	*All three*	*Any Two*	*Any Two*
Drive for improvement	**Teamworking**	**Transformational leadership**	**Strategic thinking**
1 Creates improvements	1 Contributes to the team	1 Keeps people informed	1 Stands back to see patterns
2 Sets and works to meet challenging goals	2 Expresses positive expectations of the team	2 Promotes organisational effectiveness	2 Uses models
3 Weighs costs and benefits	3 Secures contributions	3 Tends the team	3 Uses big pictures
4 Takes risks for performance gains	4 Builds team identity and spirit	4 Gains commitment to a competing vision	4 Introduces new thinking
Initiative	**Impact and influence**	**Holding people accountable**	**Information seeking**
1 Seeks opportunities and sorts out problems	1 Takes actions to persuade	1 Establishes clear expectations	1 Asks questions
2 Thinks and acts ahead	2 Calculates an impact	2 Sets limits	2 Digs deeper
3 Prepares for future opportunities	3 Influences indirectly	3 Demands delivery	3 Researches
4 Acts now to achieve a long-term payoff	4 Uses sophisticated influencing	4 Challenges performance	4 Uses systems
Personal conviction	**Understanding others**	**Developing potential**	**Analytic thinking**
1 Expresses an independent view	1 Reads body language	1 Shows how	1 Breaks down problems
2 Is authoritative	2 Understands meanings	2 Provides tangible support	2 Sees implications
3 Rises to challenges	3 Understands underlying issues	3 Gives feedback and encouragement	3 Analyses complicated problems
4 Relishes challenge	4 Understands group dynamics	4 Creates development opportunities	4 Undertakes analysis of very complex problems.

Source: The Competency Profile – Hay McBer (2000)

Over the years this approach to formal leadership has been referred to as 'situational', 'contingent' or, in reference to one particular sociological construct, as 'garbage can decision-making' (March and Olsen, 1976). The new national standards for headteachers meanwhile are aspirational in nature and are based on the notion of schools as particular types of organizations. The behaviours relating to the standards are entirely appropriate for an improving school where the inherent purpose is the raising of student achievement, in particular in relation to student performance on external tests, and where high levels of staff collaboration and mutual trust are evident.

In short, therefore, the standards will equip you to run a school that meets that specification. If you happen to be asked to do this in difficult or challenging circumstances, however, or find yourself in a school where reality is different from the public image presented at the recruitment stage, then standards are less useful with adherence to them actually becoming an encumbrance.

Leadership in Action

There is also a distinction to be made between theoretical constructs of formal leadership and leadership in action, which is not recognized in the standards that focus only on the actions of the one in charge. Leadership is actually a social interaction where the behaviours or competence of others are affected more by the leader than the leader is affected by them (Bass, 1981). This has led to the realization that leadership happens at all levels within an organization and is not just something that formal leaders do. In turn this has created the drive towards collective models of leadership, commonly known as 'distributed leadership', where the emphasis is on the formal leader harnessing and developing the leadership potential within the organization in support of its agreed purpose and aims.

The difficulty within the English school system is that whilst headteachers can devolve responsibility, and thereby increase organizational effectiveness and efficiency, they cannot devolve accountability. That means they have to accept risk as a key element of their existence and learn to live with failures that could have been avoided in the search for better leadership practice in schools. Trust in others and trust in you is built through such failures. The standards, however, are strangely reticent as regards these and other aspects of distributed leadership.

In summary, therefore, I would suggest it is impossible to have a universal set of standards as each headship is unique. As argued in previous chapters, and notably in Chapter 2, for learning to become effective the prospective and neophyte headteacher needs to build knowledge and skills along three dimensions – personally, occupationally and organizationally. My conclusion is that the national standards fixate on the occupational dimension.

The National Professional Qualification for Headship (NPQH)

So where does this leave the NPQH licensure scheme? Based as it is on the national standards you might by this time be thinking that they are not as helpful in the identification and development of headteachers as some would have you believe. Well let me make one thing absolutely clear at the beginning of this section. I am not against the NPQH, but I do have reservations about its ability to prepare you for the reality of headship. My research has shown that nothing can really prepare people for headship and it is the living of that experience that really transforms you from an aspirant to an effective headteacher, with appropriate support in the early part of headship being the critical instrumental factor in assisting that transition.

The NPQH has its place, however, and is of course now a mandatory requirement. From April, 2004, all applicants to headship have been required either to have the qualification or be registered on the programme; by 2009 you will not be able to apply for a headship without the NPQH. Research that I have conducted (Male, 2001) and other research commissioned by the NCSL (National College for School Leadership, 2004) show that the NPQH can have a positive impact on the perceptions of candidates to engage with the demands of headship. It must be remembered, however, that both pieces of research have limitations and, in themselves, are not conclusive. Self-perception is but one measure of effectiveness and there is little other evidence to support the claim that these perceptions lead, in turn, to improved performance. Furthermore, the NCSL research falls into the trap of only investigating people's reaction to the training, development and certification, rather than asking fundamental questions about the process.

The NPQH, like most licensure schemes, operates on a fail-safe policy through the provision of a relevant curriculum and engagement with practical development opportunities, before making an assessment on the readiness of a candidate to enter headship. It stakes no claim for guaranteed performance which, as we have seen in previous chapters, is contingent on the ability of a candidate to adapt their knowledge and skills to a new leadership environment. The development of a necessary range of personal qualities is more likely to happen after appointment than during preparation, especially given the frequent absence of appropriate learning opportunities to be gained through suitable models of apprenticeship and internship. Formal preparation programmes seek, therefore, to ensure that prospective formal leaders have explored a range of relevant theory and examples of practical expertise and have been required to apply these to a practical situation. Such experiences establish a minimum standard in these aspects of headship and are thus a fail-safe system, with those who emerge with the qualification having a reasonable idea of what the job entails.

Licensure schemes should seek to guide participant learning so that a suitable body of knowledge is accumulated prior to final assessment and, ideally, extend learning into areas that provide a real challenge to the aspirant headteacher. To that extent the NPQH can be shown to be moving in the right direction in terms of building knowledge and experience. The original precept for the NPQH was that it would guarantee these criteria by demanding every candidate went through each stage of the process, with the tutors and facilitators being contractually required to follow a prescribed script in formal training sessions.

It was realized soon afterwards that this was demanding too much of the better candidates – those close to headship – and revisions were made in 1999 to allow alternative routes through to completion. Those unable to demonstrate sufficient knowledge, experience and expertise were to undertake a full programme lasting up to three years (Route 1) starting with the Access programme, which consisted mainly of a suite of on-line learning modules for each key area of headship. Candidates deemed to have suitable knowledge, experience and expertise were offered the Development stage (with training), lasting no longer than one year and consisting of planned training sessions and school based experiences (Route 2). Those close to headship were admitted to the Development stage (without training), requiring them to demonstrate their capability through the assessment of school based activity and to attend a 48-hour residential programme that focused on strategic leadership and vision (Route 3). All candidates are subject to the final stage which includes the 48-hour residential session and a one day final skills assessment conducted at one of the NCSL's regional centres.

Candidates for the NPQH are thus required to make application to join the programme at an appropriate point, with the emphasis being on them to substantiate their claim. The on-line application process, supported by statements from one or two key professionals who have had first-hand experience of their work, asks them to nominate their desired route. Assessors appointed by the NCSL's contractors then evaluate the application either to confirm the self-assessment or recommend an alternative route which, in some cases, is for a shortened programme as some candidates underestimate their own abilities. The difficulty in differentiating between claims for Route 1 and Route 2 led the NCSL to once more review the process and plan to remove the Access programme altogether, with the cohort applying in late 2005 having the last chance to undertake this route. The NCSL review concluded that the introduction of the Leading from the Middle programme (LftM) had raised the capability of phase co-ordinators and subject leaders to see the bigger picture and to contribute to a school's strategic processes. What was needed now was a bridging programme after LftM that allowed aspirant headteachers to build the necessary knowledge, experience and expertise before applying for the NPQH. That programme is due to be introduced in 2006.

In terms of knowledge it can be demonstrated through this analysis that the routes to NPQH certification do have the potential to provide a suitable curriculum for potential headteachers. As a practising academic and active researcher, I would always like to see more in the way of substantiated theory forming a part of this curriculum rather than the application of conventional wisdom, and for there to be more in the way of active debate about the rigour of that knowledge – but by the very nature of my profession I am obliged to say that! I have already argued in Chapter 3, however, that the NPQH does not provide a rigorous curriculum in terms of practical experience (in keeping with most similar licensure schemes). The consequence for those seeking to be effective headteachers as early in their career as possible is that they should look at the range of learning opportunities they could engage in before taking up post, as well as the ones they must engage in, in order to develop potential for formal school leadership that moves them beyond the NPQH.

The National College for School Leadership

The National College for School Leadership (or NCSL) took principal responsibility for the development of school leadership in England from September 2000. The brainchild of a new Labour government, the college serves the nation state of England and is unique in terms of other school leadership development systems world wide.

Although the college remit has been broad in scope and subject to continuous change since its inception, it has consistently sustained three main aims:

- to provide a national focus for school leadership and research;
- to be a driving force for world class leadership in schools and the wider education service;
- to be a provider and promoter of excellence, a major resource for schools, a catalyst for innovation and a focus for national and international debate on school leadership issues.

The college is in receipt of direct funding from the government and is jointly responsible with the Training and Development Agency for the professional development of the full range of the school workforce, from support staff through to senior leadership team. For the period 2005–06 the college received funding of just under £100m for four streams of activity: the provision of leadership development programmes; collaborative work on national strategic initiatives; innovation, research and development; and infrastructure costs. With a change of priorities, and the need to work more collaboratively, total funding for 2006–07 was set at £74m, although this reduction should be considered as a realignment of funding to other agencies rather than a reduced investment in the college. Reductions on infrastructure costs were to be in line with the same requirements of other government bodies, meaning that funding decisions were logistical and left the core priorities of the college largely intact.

The college is unique in that it is both an agency and a physical entity. Its headquarters are located on a university campus in purpose-built accommodation that provides both a working base for the employees and a residential training facility, equipped with state-of-the-art technology. The college was a policy initiative driven by the desire to raise school standards, but is also viewed as the product of previous experience of leadership development at a national level. What distinguishes it from previous investment in the professional development of senior staff in schools is the combination of agency role, residential training provision and an investment in open learning. Earlier government investment in school leadership development over the previous five decades had seen all such provision, but it had never been brought together as the sole responsibility of a single agency. Developments in ICT and the Internet are considered by a well-placed adviser to be major contributing factors in the government decision to invest heavily in the college as its primary vehicle for improving school leadership (Bolam, 2004).

The advent of enhanced communication through electronic means opens the possibility of supporting an audience of school based practitioners that amounts to over 100,000 individuals in formal leadership and management positions in England's schools. As a result the college has developed web-based materials that make it one of the most popular resources for school leaders, with MORI research indicating that by 2005 around 73 per cent of headteachers were regular visitors to its site.

NCSL in Action

The main focus of activity from the college in the early years of its existence has been to support those in formal leadership positions in schools as they readily admit that the sheer volume of those who engage in leadership activity would militate against making effective provision for a potentially vast audience of teachers and support staff (Southworth, 2004). There is emphasis within the college's current corporate plan on building leadership capacity both across the school system and within schools, although it is equally recognized that this objective can only be achieved in collaboration. To that end, therefore, the college now works in close collaboration with other agencies through various strategic initiatives, such as the Primary Leadership Programme, Strategic Leadership of ICT and the London Challenge.

Core activity is heavily focused on programmes and research. Programmes have been developed to match the five categories of school leadership identified by their own Think Tank, commissioned in 2001, and contained within the Leadership Development Framework published by the college in the following year:

- *Emergent leaders*: teachers who are beginning to take on management and leadership responsibilities, including heads of department and subject coordinators;
- *Established leaders*: experienced leaders who do not intend to pursue headship, including assistant and deputy headteachers;
- *Entry to headship*: those preparing for their first headship and for newly appointed headteachers;
- *Advanced leaders*: experienced headteachers looking to refresh themselves and update their skills;
- *Consultant leaders*: experienced headteachers and other school leaders who are ready to further develop their training, mentoring and coaching skills.

The NCSL's research and innovation are driven by a stated desire to bridge a perceived gap between practice and research and are manifested through a range of strategies designed to engage practitioners. Research into best practice is analysed and investment is made into practitioner enquiry, involvement and voice. The college has produced and continues to produce a knowledge base designed to inform school leadership and to promote dialogue between practitioners and scholars. Large numbers of publications have emerged from this activity, readily available on the college web-site, consisting of practitioner reports from research associates (usually headteachers) or commissioned summaries of research into key topics in the field. A sensible balance is felt to have been achieved between this approach and more fundamental research has continued to have been undertaken by professional researchers funded by other agencies or foundations (Bolam, 2004).

The NCSL and Headteachers

The NCSL thus seeks to support headteachers at all stages of their preparation, induction and continuing professional development, principally through three key programme areas. For entry to headship they run the NPQH and HIP and for advanced leaders they provide the LPSH. Professional development is something more than certification or formal programmes, however, so the provision, maintenance and extension of a knowledge base through its activities in research and innovation can also be judged as supportive of headteacher development. Equally the Consultant Leader programme and the International Placements for Headteachers (IPH), run in conjunction with the British Council, have made a significant impact in terms of career and personal development.

The level of engagement with the NCSL by the nation's headteachers depends upon which view you take of such activities. A MORI poll of serving headteachers conducted in 2005 showed nearly 90 per cent of headteachers to be aware of the college's purpose, with 80 per cent of those surveyed saying they had participated in a college activity. Smaller levels of direct involvement are demonstrated through other measures, however, which show that there are sufficient NPQH graduates for about half of the nation's 23,000 maintained schools and that a similar proportion of serving headteachers has taken part in the LPSH programme. Meanwhile, HIP has recruited just over 1200 participants since its inception to join the 5000 or so who had participated in HEADLAMP, the previous induction programme. Other programmes and initiatives similarly boast largish numbers, but do not demonstrate coverage of the headteacher population.

These figures do not of themselves suggest anything significant about the college's ability to make an impact across the entire school system and are probably more indicative of the ability and enthusiasm of the nation's headteachers to engage in the activities provided. Evaluations of the programmes and their impact consistently demonstrate high levels of satisfaction with outcomes, both at a personal and systemic level. The Chief Inspector of Schools views school leadership and management as being incrementally better in successive years, with only a very small proportion of the nation's headteachers adjudged to be unsatisfactory or poor in his most recently published report (Ofsted, 2005). It is safe to assume that the college has made a contribution to that improved level of headteacher performance, although questions still remain over the level of impact across the whole system.

The Impact of the NCSL

When asked to comment on the efficacy of the French Revolution of 1789, Chairman Mao Tse Tung of the People's Republic of China replied in the late 1960s by saying "it's too early to tell". The same general assessment can be applied to the NCSL at this stage of its life. Like all non-departmental government agencies in the UK, the college is subject to review every five years and came out of its 2005 End-to-End Review reasonably well. There was encouragement for the college to exhibit greater precision, discipline, outcome-focus and depth in its work and a recommendation that activities should be both evidence based and proportionate to their capacity.

Implied criticisms contained in that report pale into insignificance beside those levelled at predecessor agencies. After ten years of investment of countless millions of pounds in the 1980s' programme of management development (for example, the one term training opportunities (OTTO) and 20 day development programmes for school based senior staff) only 11 per cent of the target population had been reached (School Management Task Force, 1990). Meanwhile the Teacher Training Agency, in its own five year review of 1999, was told it had 'made few friends' in the process of conducting its business (Department for Education and Employment, 1999). The NCSL got off lightly in comparison and probably rightly so.

Any concerns that remain, therefore, are not about intent or enthusiasm, but about coverage. We can assume, for example, that the preparation of future generations of headteachers is reasonably well catered for (even given my concerns voiced in Chapter 2 over appropriate learning experiences for aspirant headteachers). There should be sufficient participants in pre-headship development programmes and NPQH graduates, by dint of the legislative directive, to meet the demands of the system in the future. Worryingly, however, the participation in early headship programmes, particularly HIP, is below half the target population. Given that the early part of headship is critical in developing personal effectiveness, as demonstrated in Chapters 2 and 6, it is of some concern that so few headteachers are taking full advantage of the support mechanisms available to them.

In part this low take-up can be demonstrated to be the lack of a database which identified new appointments and in part an artefact of confusion within the NCSL as to both the purpose of the HIP programme and the contemporaneous marketing of a competing programme – New Visions. The good news is that HIP and New Visions are to be combined in a revised early headship programme. The bad news is that the NCSL still does not know who is eligible and consequently makes participation voluntary. For serving headteachers the opportunities for the LPSH are set at about 1200 participants per year with a further 350 expected to undertake international visits in the IPH programme and similar numbers to be paired with business leaders through the Partnerships in Leadership (PIL) programme or to become Consultant Leaders. Whilst the volume of this provision is laudable it still means that the majority of head-teachers are not getting regular access to the NCSL-funded provision.

What does this Mean to Me as a Headteacher?

Let us assume that you will have already passed through the preparation of headship programme, including the NPQH. Any other route to headship is by now precluded to you or no longer relevant in the maintained sector. That means you should really be looking at how you can best benefit from the remaining NCSL provision.

Clearly, the NCSL's knowledge base is proving not only to be reasonably comprehensive but is also providing effective support for headteachers as a source of information. Their figures show a 55 per cent increase in use of its electronic resource base since its inception and the college recorded over 80,000 unique visitors to the web-site every month during 2003 (Southworth, 2004). The site can be considered as the most effective way of updating your knowledge which, especially if used interactively, can make a significant con-tribution to your own professional development and to school improvement. You should be using it regularly (available at www.ncsl.org.uk).

The most disappointing level of engagement with the NCSL's provision is with the entry to headship programmes of such as HIP and New Visions. The only excuse for not registering for HIP (or its pending replacement) that can be offered by a headteacher appointed to their first headship is that they are too busy to think about their continuing professional devel-opment. Certainly that assumption can be made in relation to the discus-sion conducted in Chapters 2 and 6, but such an excuse can only hold good for the first confused stage of headship. Even then, evidence shows that usually the best level of support for beginning headteachers is from a mentor and there is an element of funding for this contained within the version of HIP that was current at the time of writing. To my mind, as a beginning headteacher you are duty bound to register for this funding and to make sure you access all relevant support funded through the scheme.

As an effective headteacher, however, you are also duty bound to take full responsibility for your continuing professional development at all stages of your career. That means you should be looking to access all possible funding sources that will support that aim including, of course, any provi-sion made by the college for serving headteachers. As will become more evident once you have read Chapter 6, once you have made the decision to be an effective headteacher your mission will almost certainly be directed toward creating and sustaining a more effective learning environment in your school. A key component of such an environment is a willingness by the headteacher to demonstrate they are a learner as much as a provider.

5 | Applying for headship

I would not be offended if you were to consider it superfluous for me to be offering advice and guidance on how to apply for a job at this stage of your working life. Nevertheless, my research shows that the majority of aspirant headteachers rush into their application, often more enamoured with the thought of headship than in examining closely the implications of a particular post. There are two key components of the application process and most attention is usually given by an applicant to presenting themselves in the best way possible in order to be the chosen one.

Jobs are contractual obligations on behalf of both the employer and the employee, however, so equal attention should be given to the choice of school. Ultimately effective headship is contingent on your compatibility to the school community and vice versa, so time should be spent evaluating the school in relation to your ambition to be successful. Consequently this chapter looks at all aspects of applying for headship up to the point where you are offered the post and begins by examining how you can present yourself as the best choice for your chosen school.

Making Yourself the Best Choice

By now licensure is required for virtually all those who seek to apply for the principal leadership position in schools. There are exceptions and headship of an independent school, for example, still requires neither licence nor teaching qualification, whilst serving headteachers in England's maintained schools will not need to retrospectively gain the NPQH in order to apply to subsequent schools. For the rest, however, there is a universal requirement to gain appropriate and relevant qualifications in order to be considered for the position. Generally these days that means you need to gain the professional certification relevant to your school system rather than academic qualifications that may have been deemed equivalent in former days. The outcome of this move to licensure is that you can now be assured that this is the starting point for application, rather than an indication of your individual capability for a specific job. Applicants for headship will require, therefore, a unique selling point (USP), usually comprising attributes and traits that make them stand out from the crowd.

As a prospective candidate for headship, therefore, you need to be aware of the attributes that distinguish you from other possible candidates and be able to use these in pursuit of your application to a particular institution. I recently heard a leading figure from a head-hunting company based in the city of London's financial district talking about the necessary elements that he and his recruitment team sought in a prospective candidate for a key leadership role. The possible contenders, he claimed, exhibited four factors: personal values that matched the organization seeking the new leader; an appropriate range of skills and competences for the job in question; a track record of achievement in similar or comparable roles; and a final, killer, qualification that he labelled 'chemistry'.

By this I assumed he was alluding to the same type of 'chemistry' that is aligned to special relationships such as couples in love or, more impersonally, as can be seen between actors who work well together or sports teams who have superseded all realistic expectations of their combined talents. There is a danger, at this point, of allocating mystical qualities or unknown factors to the equation that remove the control of such mutually productive relationships beyond your sphere of influence. I do not happen to believe in notions of happy coincidence or fate that are total in nature, however, and remain convinced that such relationships can be engendered as much as being an artefact of circumstance. Undoubtedly there are headteachers who through serendipitous circumstances have found themselves in the right job for them and good luck to them, but such fortunate circumstances cannot be guaranteed so you need to work on your image and make sure that you exhibit the qualities that are attractive to potential employers.

Personal Values

I have already talked about the identification of personal values in Chapter 3 and have returned to them time and again throughout this book. These values represent your beliefs and underwrite the actions with which you feel comfortable. Although you may be given the opportunity to present some indication of your values in the written application, it is at the selection process where the clarity of your value set will be examined and evaluated against those held explicitly and implicitly by the members of the appointing panel (who are representative, of course, of the school community). It is an invaluable technique in the selection process, therefore, to be able to provide examples of your values in action, rather than merely to offer abstract views or statements of intent. Try to offer examples where you have successfully resolved a situation or an issue in accord with your stated values. Also recognize, however, that taking on a headship will inevitably place you in positions where those values are challenged and, occasionally, compromised in support of an effective decision. Examples of this personal conflict and successful resolution should also be developed (even if they are not always used).

Competence and Skills

Having the requisite professional qualifications for the job is only the starting point for demonstrating your competence, defined in the previous chapter as the ability to undertake an aspect of a job effectively and efficiently. As an applicant for headship you will need to be able to show a range of competences and requisite skills that are appropriate to the job. Invariably much of this profile can be evidenced through your practical experience, but more of that below. At this point you should be looking to demonstrate how you have engaged in formal development activities that distinguish you from other applicants.

Let us take the likely situation in England which will emerge by 2009. By that time all applicants to headship in maintained schools will have to have completed the NPQH before submitting their application. Invariably they will have successfully completed the nationally devised steps along the way (the Leading from the Middle programme and the NPQH Access programme or its replacement). In some instances these applicants will also have been 'Fast Track' teachers on the nationally-sponsored accelerated programme towards headship. There is no gradation of these qualifications, so what makes you different? Imagine the scene facing the school governing body as they attempt to sift through a pile of applications that show numerous candidates with no distinguishing characteristics. Put yourself in that position and you can see how quickly any shortlisting panel will be tempted to take account of other features within the applications.

There is no simple answer to the conundrum of being eligible for the job without being attractive, but the ability to provide evidence of in-service professional development wider than the minimum requirement will undoubtedly help. The most obvious example of extended commitment to your development is successful participation in an award bearing programme in Higher Education, although equal value can be accrued through other awarding bodies. Such achievement shows you have committed yourself to furthering your education and skills and have done so whilst also holding down a full-time job. Sustained engagement in non-accredited professional development programmes and events will also hold you in good stead, particularly if you can demonstrate a pattern designed to build your capability for future roles. Remember that you are aiming to step up at this point, so activities designed to make you better at your current job are not so valuable as those where you can be shown to be preparing yourself for a future career.

Recording and presenting evidence of your continued development are required, so consideration needs to be given to this activity when preparing your application for a headship. In many ways this should be second nature as teachers are now encouraged throughout their career to maintain a portfolio of evidence to sustain their claim for advancement through competence, except at this final stage. In England, for example, trainee teachers, teachers passing through to higher pay scales and NPQH participants now all need to maintain and present a portfolio of valued practical experience to support their application for the relevant transition. In other words it is normal, expected practice and yet few maintain such an evidence base for their indirect needs, limiting their efforts to statutory requirements.

The message here is quite clear – keep your profile up to date. Draw strategically on this data, however, as there is nothing so damaging to an application as information overkill. Look to see how your formal development experiences can be shown to be relevant to the job in question and synthesize accordingly into a simple statement. The last thing you should do is send in your collection of ring binders containing every known detail of every CPD event you have ever attended!

Track Record

By the very nature of the job it is impossible for those applying for their first headship position to be able to demonstrate anything other than potential, where those who are applying for second or subsequent headships can point to previous successes. No applicant's profile will be an exact match, however, given the unique characteristics of each school community. Selection panels will be looking for a close fit, therefore, between previous experience and the anticipated demands of the new job. As an applicant your first key task is to identify where you have been directly responsible for effecting change in your current or previous roles. It is astonishing how many people can point to involvement in leadership and management decision making rather than instrumentality, something I have noticed regularly when reviewing applications for entry to the NPQH. So what are the issues on which you have led successfully?

Your second task is to then map your experience of successful leadership on to the new job. If the school is in serious need of a focused improvement effort, for example, can you show how you have led the drive to improvement in your previous existence and thus apply those skills to this challenge? Some demands are less obvious, however, and to present yourself as the best candidate you will need to have carried out some research on the school to which you are applying, but more of that below.

Chemistry

I have already alluded to the nebulous nature of this concept, but it will come down to the personal qualities you are able to demonstrate in your application and during the selection process. This is where you need to demonstrate your individuality and extended skills. Selection panels are looking for a variety of clues that indicate you are the person for the job and often the criteria they employ can remain hidden, or even be unfairly biased. A survey conducted in 2004 on behalf of the NCSL in England, for example, showed that half of women applying for headship in a secondary school experienced overt and covert sexism during the selection process and, although the proportion was smaller, there were still 30 per cent who felt they had been treated similarly in primary schools (Coleman, 2005). Similar findings relating to the ethnicity of applicants have also been recorded. Too many governors, it seems, have an image of the headteacher that corresponds to the national stereotype of formal leadership explored in Chapter 1 of this book. In England, therefore, they are typically expecting a man and preferably one who can have a commanding physical presence. There is little that can be done at an individual level to counter such overt barriers to appointment, but it is the more covert approaches that need to be monitored as you present yourself as a candidate.

You should be able to exhibit a degree of control over some of the selection process through your behaviour and appearance in order to adapt their ideal image to match your self-image. Most schools are looking for a reassuring figure to adopt the symbolic role that is so vital to organizational leadership, so a calm sense of authority, underwritten by assertiveness, is normally the ideal mode of behaviour during the selection process. Personal appearance can be an issue, especially if you do not adopt a conventional mode of dress. The real issue, however, is the way in which you interact with members of the school community during the selection process. Never underestimate the importance of any interaction. I once lost a job because I had failed to impress some people as I was shown round the school – so much for the calm, quiet, watchful mode of my behaviour as I saved myself for the main interview later!

The key to your success in this regard will be your ability to identify your strengths and apply them to the situation in order to achieve a rapport. This is a process closely aligned to the principle of emotional intelligence, understanding yourself and others, as reported in Chapter 2. Hopefully you will already have a realistic image of yourself by the time you apply for headship and will need to be able to think quickly during the selection process to present this image in line with your interpretation of the panel's expectations and aspirations. There is an argument here, however, about being truthful as then not only do you never have to remember what you have said, but there should be a greater chance of reconciling your substantial self with you situational self once you have taken up post (as discussed in Chapter 2). In other words, being yourself may be the best bet to achieving the right chemical equation.

Seeking the Job to Apply For

At the beginning of the twenty-first century we are looking at a seller's market. There is a shortage of suitably qualified people, nationally and internationally, who are prepared to put themselves forward as applicants for one of the most challenging jobs the school system – headship. It may not always be this way as circumstances may change, either because the politicization of the job recedes thus making the job more attractive, or because the structure of governance and management changes radically thus reducing the number of headships available. As is stands, however, applications for the role of formal school leader have plummeted world wide and interest in the job of headteacher in England is at an all time low at the time of writing. What is clear is that the financial attractiveness of moving to headship is not a major factor, especially in primary schools, and it is personal motivation that is driving potential applicants. We are talking here about the need for achievement, significance and belonging as opposed to pay and benefits. Typically you can afford to be a little choosy, therefore, in which job you apply for, and do bear in mind findings from research which show that too many headteachers are attracted by the notion of the job rather than the reality. Choosing a school to apply to is thus an option for many aspirant headteachers, although we must recognize that in a minority of cases it can be the school that identifies the potential headteacher. In those instances the preferred headteacher will probably be known to the school community already, either as an existing member of staff or a well respected figure from the local school system.

My research shows that a major consideration in the process of choosing a school is the potential effect on the applicant's family life. Data from national surveys show that over 90 per cent of men who were headteachers were both married and had children, where 67 per cent of women headteachers were married of whom 53 per cent had children (Coleman, 2005). Very few headteachers were free, therefore, of immediate family concerns and this obviously has a marked influence as regards the geographical area in which applications for headship can be directed. For aspirant headteachers with children of school age, there are only a few windows of opportunity available to them for relocation without seriously compromising the continuity of their own children's school experience. Most choice, therefore, is constrained by your own daily commuting range, which only you can determine.

The only words of advice I would offer in this regard is that your school is far enough away to ensure you have a private life outside school hours and that you have time to think yourself out of the job when you travel home on a daily basis. I have seen painful examples, particularly in small town USA, where the principal has no opportunity to be any other person in their private life, including having to cut their lawn whilst dressed formally as a principal – I do not exaggerate!

The next most likely criterion to employ to assist your choice is the match between your personal values and the value base that underpins the school in its current mode. Assuming your value base is secure, or that you are robust enough to withstand regular challenges to your beliefs, you still need to be a little discriminating in your assessment of the school in action. Many are the schools I have seen where the rhetoric of public announcement is not matched by the reality of experience. There is often a gap between the public image and the actual daily existence that needs to be explored before you commit yourself to the cause. This is the point where you need to do your research to find some of the inside story.

Some evidence is always available in the public domain, such as inspection reports, and the school will have a range of published information, especially marketing and recruitment materials. To gain an insight into the reality of practice, however, you may need to dig a little deeper. A preliminary visit to the local area may be necessary, particularly if you are not local yourself. Just viewing the outside of the school and visiting some local amenities can provide a wealth of information. Be aware I am not talking about undercover work here, so I am not expecting you to engage in some form of clandestine behaviour! I am really recommending that you familiarize yourself with the physical nature of the school community. Undoubtedly, however, the best way to find out the true story is to talk to people who are either members of the school community or closely associated with it – not an easy task if you are a stranger, but it may be possible that you have some relevant contacts who can provide you with a view of the school in operation.

By the time you arrive for the final selection process, therefore, you should have gained some knowledge that extends beyond that provided in the application pack. What you should be trying to do with this research is to build a vision of the challenges and opportunities that may await you if you are successful with your application. A number of these suppositions and predictions can then be checked out during the selection process and it is for you to remember that this is a two-way interchange. The penalties for not undertaking this advance reconnaissance may be long term and painful. I know of one headteacher, for example, who took on the job only to find a substantial hole in the budget which meant that virtually his first action was to make several teaching assistants redundant. As most such employees are also closely associated with the local school community you can imagine the impact this action had on this headteacher's reputation. This type of situation is by no means the most dramatic example of issues that can be conveniently hidden during the application and selection process, so you would always be advised to do your homework.

Applying for a Job

You will always be required to submit a formal application and in most school systems there will be a standard application process. Generally this will consist of an application form which allows you to present your personal details, including your qualifications, together with a range of other relevant documentation. As a seasoned teacher you will have met many such situations before, so this type of requirement will not come as much of a surprise. In school systems underpinned by well run personnel services, however, you can expect to see the opportunity provided for you to demonstrate the appropriateness of your application to the particular job. Most LEAs, for example, have employed robust systems of selection for maintained schools that allow them to distinguish between applicants in a totally transparent way. Usually this desire on their behalf is satisfied by describing the job in terms of essential and desirable characteristics. Your key task in preparing your application will be to match your experience and expertise to those characteristics so that you can demonstrate that, on paper at least, you are an eligible candidate.

Formal school systems are generally very rigorous in this regard as they are bound by relevant employment legislation and accountable to other agencies. Notions of fairness must be evident and there are legal and political requirements regarding a lack of discrimination in appointment procedures. Not always will you find such rigour, however, but the principle of demonstrating your compatibility with the job is always best answered through identifying essential and desirable characteristics and preparing your application accordingly. Where these characteristics are not explicit, your task is more difficult as you will have to identify the implicit expectations of the prospective employer through other means. The key fact to remember, especially in formal systems, is that an application that matches the essential and desired characteristics should lead to you being listed as one of the possible finalists. Furthermore, no additional criteria can then be introduced during the selection process as this would contravene the legislative and accountability requirements of the employer.

Inevitably you will need to qualify your application with the evidence you supply in addition to the factual information required to complete the application form. How you furnish that information will be one of the key factors that govern your selection for further consideration. Traditionally, in

England, people have supplied a letter of application to supplement the factual information provided, although there are other means of providing further detail. The trick is to make this further information entirely focused on the job you are applying for. That rules out supplying your entire curriculum vitae, as parts of that profile will not be applicable to the job for which you are applying. It also rules out the 'form' letter, especially where you may inadvertently forget to change the name of the school. Unquestionably you will be preparing real and possible applications for a number of schools, so careful editing of the material that could be included is essential so that each application is individually prepared. Similarly a high level of proof reading of the final application is critical as, notwithstanding any silly mistakes, your spelling and grammatical errors will swiftly take you out of contention.

Remember, you are applying for the senior educationalist position in a school and people expect you to be a paragon of virtue in terms of your literacy skills. I have to admit to being astonished when I see spelling mistakes from aspirant headteachers and it seems I am joined in that view by most governing bodies. Get a trusted family member or friend to check your applications for errors and omissions, especially if they have an excellent grip of language. Do not let a split infinitive or a misplaced apostrophe stand between you and the job you desire.

The style of writing you adopt for this aspect of your application will also have an impact on the selection panel, in addition to the content. What the selectors will be hoping for is a succinct explanation that demonstrates you are the person most likely to meet their aspirations for a new headteacher. Consequently you should be seeking to weave your experience and expertise around the essential and desirable characteristics of the job, but keep it just short enough so that they can read it fairly quickly and then compare your evidence to their checklist of characteristics. It is useful to put in some statements of belief, but these should be backed up by evidence of those beliefs being enacted in practice, rather than a set of pious or aspirational statements. Do not over or under state your claims as these will be examined in the subsequent selection processes. Do not, for example, claim to be fluent in a different language when really all you can manage is the construction of a reasonable question but then cannot understand the answer. Alternatively do not claim to have merely assisted in, say, the improvement in student test scores when they would not have been achieved without your expertise, drive and enthusiasm. For some reason relating to a misguided sense of nobility and a very strong cultural influence most people in England are prone to self-deprecation, having been socialized into such behaviour patterns. Now is not the time to undersell yourself.

One final thing to do before you send off your application is to check who is going to act as referee to your claims. It is very rare these days, especially in the maintained schools sector, that references are used in the selection process and are often only examined subsequently in order to satisfy the selectors that your claims and their judgement are being verified by a third party. Those who you nominate as referees need to know your professional practice well and be able to comment authoritatively on your performance in your current role and on your potential as a headteacher. Consequently you might like to give some thought to this choice early on in the application process and ensure that your preferred referees are the most appropriate ones to support your application. If you do not name a key figure who represents your current employer this will raise some concerns in the minds of those considering your application. It is always helpful, therefore, if your direct 'boss' (that is, your current headteacher, chair of governors or link adviser) can be nominated as your principal referee.

There may be good reason why this is neither possible nor practical, however, and you may well need to explain at some point why this is the case. Certainly there will be occasions where you may suspect the relationship between you and a potential referee is not of a sufficiently high quality for you to be given a fair reference. Equally, you may not wish to alert your employer that you are seeking positions elsewhere (although some potential new employers will allow you to ask that references are not taken up before the final selection process takes place). Be prepared, therefore, to answer the inevitable question that will follow the absence of your current employer as nominated referee.

One last thing. Always try to let your nominated referee know that you have named them in your application – firstly to seek their permission and secondly to gain their support. It is very discomforting for any nominated referee to be suddenly confronted with the need to supply a reference without prior notice and this may adversely affect what they say about you subsequently.

The Selection Process

Assuming there are reasonably sound personnel procedures in place, you can expect to be invited to join a shortlist of suitably qualified candidates for a final selection process if the quality of your application has been good enough to match their expectations. In most instances the final selection process these days is a combination of formal and informal procedures and activities spread across a period of time, usually two to three days. It is very rare for the traditional interview panel to be the only selection process employed, although that formal structure does still carry considerable weight, especially in the eyes of governing bodies. Typically you can now expect a number of practical activities, some informal social gatherings and some formal processes. Your behaviour in this battery of events will be judged continually by the selectors who will make use of a number of explicit and implicit criteria in reaching their final decision. Some of these processes will be unfair and you will have little control over such phenomena. The important thing to remember at the end of this process is that you were qualified to join at the outset and, if rejected, the selection process does not necessarily determine your quality as a prospective headteacher. All the final decision means is that the selection panel have agreed on who they perceive to be the best choice for their school.

You may be invited to several final selection processes, therefore, and engage in a variety of activities that are supposed to provide evidence that you are the best choice for the job. Typically, headteacher applicants in England take part in several final selection processes before being offered and accepting a job. The exceptions to this rule are where there are limited applicants or someone is persuaded to apply for a particular headship, effectively being offered the post. The image of a long-serving senior teacher in a small school springs to mind at this point, or someone who has been headhunted in order to meet a particular challenge. Legally, all headships of maintained schools in England have to be advertised nationally and are thus theoretically open appointments. The same rules do not apply to the independent sector and circumstances may be such that individuals are effectively nominated for headships within the maintained sector.

Generally most headships will be competitive, with applicants usually becoming increasingly competent as they engage in successive selection processes. You can now expect to be asked to take part in formal tests and tasks in order to provide evidence of your competence in action. These may include psychometric tests, administered before or during the final selection process, or leadership and management tasks that are required to be completed without prior notice. It is not unusual these days, for example, to be asked to make a presentation on a topic where you are only given a limited amount of time to prepare.

For those of you who have worked through formal preparation programmes, such as the NPQH, demands of this nature are unlikely to be a surprise to you as you may well have engaged in such activities during your training, but those approaching the headship from a different direction may find such demands a little intimidating. The key factor that such tasks are examining here is your ability to assimilate and present information quickly and effectively. Obviously the more skilled you are at presentation, including technical skills, the more effective you will appear at this point in the selection process, so you might like to give some thought to your personal development in this regard prior to arriving at the school.

A less defined element of the selection process is your engagement with other people during informal situations. It is best to remember that, effectively, you are on show from the moment you arrive and the most difficult thing to know is when exactly you are being judged. It may be your appearance, your manner or your behaviour that influences both the selection panel and others you meet, whose opinion may well be sought by those making the final decision. There are some obvious things to avoid during the time you make yourself available to your prospective new school (such as avoiding any alcohol offered at the informal buffet reception for governors and parents, for example), but not all social settings can be anticipated and nor can their importance be assessed from your perspective. Best, therefore, to treat all such interactions the same – with caution – and to sustain the impression of calm authority alluded to earlier in this chapter. Equally there are some classic ways to present yourself, dress being the most obvious, with the best choice normally being the conservative and traditional.

A big decision is how much to talk. You are there, after all, to present both yourself and your ideas, with talking being one of the principal vehicles available to you in that respect. There are no hard and fast rules, other than the usual parameters of not talking too much or too little and only speaking when you have something sensible or worthwhile to say. As a rule of thumb, however, you need to remember that vocal contributions may be needed more frequently than your usual pattern. As a prospective headteacher you will already have learned the value of listening in order to help you make decisions. Two ears and one mouth are normally considered the right proportion and this ratio is evident in successful leadership activity.

Now you may have to adjust that proportion inversely in order to ensure you say all you want to say and this may mean that you have to emphasize some key issues repeatedly. Most selection processes provide you with a platform to ensure that you reveal all the essential information to the panel so that their final decision is an informed one. So for some key aspects of your application make sure they know what you are offering and do not assume that information from one activity will automatically be transmitted to the final decision making process.

Accepting the Job – Reconciliation of Ambition to Reality

So, to the final decision – yours, not theirs! Do you want the job? The panel has made its decision and wants to appoint you to the job. Do you accept?

By now you should have asked all the questions you want to ask and should be close to evaluating the reality of the school against your ambition when you first applied. If the school has not measured up to your expectations you will have already made a decision either to withdraw or to accept under certain conditions. Withdrawal is always a difficult decision which, in reality, should have been addressed before this final stage. You should have known earlier this was not the job for you and acted accordingly. Also you will have almost certainly been asked at some earlier juncture of your willingness to accept the job if it were to be offered. Leaving such a decision to the end point of the selection process is not good practice, a fact commonly recognized by the withholding of expenses for those who leave the decision so late. Consequently at this point you are only investigating the terms and conditions under which you will accept.

There are a number of issues you need to resolve before verbally indicating your intention to accept. You need to check the pay, the annual review procedure and options for your continuing professional development. Typically there will be well-established routines for assimilation to normal pay scales and for annual review procedures, so often this is just a case of carefully reading through the details for confirmation. It may be that you want to negotiate your pay, although that is a matter for you alone. Just make sure you do confirm your salary, remembering that all good selection procedures should allow you the opportunity to ask any questions you would like answered before the end of the process.

It is less common for headteacher applicants to enquire about support for their continuing professional development, but I would recommend you bring this up as well. An effective headteacher will seek to continually extend their knowledge and skills, with some of this development requiring the apportionment of resources in terms of time and/or funding. Remember that time and money spent on your continuing education are valuable investments on behalf of the school as you will need to be an effective learner if you are to lead a learner-centred school. Quality learning opportunities should be available to you as much as any other member of the school community and if you don't ask, you don't get!

It is unlikely you will be verbally offered the job as employers are reluctant to make offers until they have checked your references and police record. This is good personnel practice and a written offer will follow in due course. When you put your signature on that contract you will have accepted the job and become headteacher designate of your chosen school. Now all you have to do is prepare yourself for the day when you move into your new school – a wait that will become one of increasing excitement and anticipation.

6 | Entering headship

People entering headship have to reconcile their ambition with the reality they find in their new school, a process that may require them to adjust their behaviours and attitudes to match their new circumstances. Most people find the early stages of a new job challenging as they come to terms with the demands and expectations of a new workplace environment. The process is more difficult for headteachers who are expected to be capable and effective immediately on taking up post. After all, that is why they have been appointed, isn't it?

We already know from the discussion in Chapter 2 that entry into headship is potentially prone to a number of expectations about you as formal leader of the school. Hopefully you will have investigated the school as best you can before applying and accepting the post, as suggested in the previous chapter. If you have done so you will have formed the view that you consider the personal needs and aspirations you have for the job can be fulfilled. This, of course, is your ideal scenario and in your mind's eye you are already a long way toward the reconciliation of your substantial and situational self, the position where you are comfortable, confident and competent in your headship. Research shows, however, that rarely is that idealism reached in practice and the first six months especially represent a steep learning curve. For first-time headteachers there is a range of other issues which also complicates induction and early effectiveness and this will be explored separately later in the chapter.

Sense-Making

The early days of any new job are characterized by a period of sense-making, a period of intense learning as the new member develops a cognitive map, or mental model, of the organization. For the formal leader this not only involves a process of orientation to the organization but also includes a process of evaluation – an assessment of staff, understanding where the problems lie and establishing priorities (Gabarro, 1987). This period is also governed by the needs of the organization. Those organizations with 'turn round' requirements, for example, need direct and dynamic leadership action from the start, whereas that process of assimilation can be extended for organizations that are in equilibrium or a phase of improvement. Yet whatever the perceived or actual state of the organization, there will be a period of cognitive dissonance as personal aspirations and expectations are tempered by the demands of the job and the organization. Successive studies of school leadership in several countries and school systems have shown this first phase frequently requires the individual to reappraise their ambitions and to make a rapid adjustment in order to match the reality of the job in action before being able to effect real change (see for example Weindling and Earley, 1987; Parkay and Hall, 1992; Day and Bakioglu, 1996; Reeves et al., 1998).

This is the period of personal transition which, in Chapter 2, was linked with organizational needs and demonstrated to be a lonely route, particularly for those new to headship. The point of resolution with these personal challenges is when you feel confident and competent in the job, by which time you will have engaged in much reflection and internal debate in realigning your values with the system or vice versa.

At the point of entry to the new school your personal beliefs will be placed under pressure by the actions of those for whom you have responsibility and by those to whom you are accountable. The state of idealism you occupied in anticipation of taking up the job will be challenged, therefore, by the behaviour of others as well as the attributes of the organization. At a personal level this often leads to a need to reappraise in search of reassurance, not an easy thing to do when you are trying to simultaneously assimilate yourself to new systems and procedures.

Weindling (2000) has synthesized the research findings of his own investigations and the work of others in the field to define stages of headteacher development. This analysis has led him to conclude that people first engage in a period of Entry and Encounter in order to develop an understanding of the complexities of the situation, the people, the problems and the school culture. The danger here is that the wants and needs of the organization can become central in determining headteacher behaviour, as the inherent conservatism present in most social systems competes with any desire for change. Consequently you will need to exhibit your authority and demonstrate an independence of thought that will allow you time to take stock without becoming naturalized. You are, after all, the symbolic leader of a fairly autonomous organization and carry with you implicit expectations inherent in society, the school system and (probably) the school community that you are capable of being decisive and charismatic.

Initial crises and subsequent events permitting, as a new headteacher you are recommended, however, to experience a complete annual cycle of school events and learn about the strengths and weaknesses of the staff before commencing any major reshaping activities. In many ways the first year of headship needs to be treated like the garden of a new house. You might move in and know there are weeds and undergrowth that need clearing, but you don't know what is under the surface. By early spring you will know where the bulbs are, however, and can cut your grass confident in the knowledge of the location of naturalized spring flowers. By mid-summer you will have discovered which perennials have survived and the full extent of any shrubbery or tree canopy. By the end of the year you will know if you have any late blooming foliage, all of which allows you to make plans for the next year confident in the knowledge of how your actions will affect the long-term health of the plants you choose to keep.

Decision making during the first stage of your headship ideally needs to be cautious, therefore, perhaps focusing on those issues either where an obvious solution offers itself or where the impact will not have long-term or irrevocable consequences. The art of decision making is to buy enough time to make an informed and considered choice, but not to overly prevaricate. This was labelled as the creation of decision-space in Chapter 2, where it was pointed out that this runs contrary to the implicit expectation of a national culture where decisiveness is seen as a trait to be applauded. So you are looking for a small, but significant, example of your ability to make decisions that demonstrate your authority. Probably the best way to do that is to respond to decision-making opportunities where you can demonstrate your values in action. These are the places where you can show the school community your non-negotiable positions; the point where you can say, metaphorically if needs be, "there is no way I will be able to support ... because I believe that to be wrong." Such actions will allow you to establish your moral standpoints and demonstrate authority without necessarily committing you to any specific action.

By the end of the first year headteachers have usually developed a deeper understanding of key issues and begin to challenge the taken-for-granted nature of the school, although it must be kept in mind that this time frame is not always set in stone, especially where there are deep seated or complex issues which may lead to the first stage taking several years. Weindling (2000) refers to the period of incumbency between Entry and Taking Hold as the 'honeymoon period', characterized by a spell of leniency in terms of staff response to change initiated by a new headteacher, although this was not universally true with many negative situations also being reported during this stage. By the end of the Entry and Encounter stage, however, a headteacher is no longer 'new' and members of the school community have learned about their strengths and weaknesses. With the expectations of the headteacher and the school community becoming more realistic, the process of reshaping should begin.

First-time Headships

Although all newly appointed headteachers experience, to some degree, the issues emerging from the Entry and Encounter stage, those entering headship for the first time have the additional burden of managing their personal transition into an occupation that is new to them. These challenges have been fairly well documented in contemporary research and have been best summarized in a review commissioned by the National College for School Leadership, which demonstrated the following key issues as being relevant to first-time headteachers appointed in England:

• feelings of professional isolation and loneliness;
• dealing with the legacy, practice and style of the previous headteacher;
• dealing with multiple tasks, managing time and priorities;
• managing the school budget;
• dealing with (for example supporting, warning, dismissing) ineffective staff;
• implementing new government initiatives, notably new curricula or school improvement projects;
• problems with school buildings and site management.

(Hobson et al., 2003)

Although these issues are consistent and can be expected to manifest themselves with all new headships, the key point for first-time headteachers is to make the transformation from participant in major decisions to the final arbiter of which choice to make. In making this transition to headship about one in seven of the respondents to my national survey of headteachers took the opportunity to comment on the isolated, varied and frightening nature of their early experiences in headship in their responses to the open questions in the questionnaire. Contributing to those feelings were fear of the unknown, the levels of responsibility envisaged for the new job by self and others, the lack of understanding from others as to the intensity of the job and a growing realization by individuals that the same job demanded more from them than was encompassed in the terms and conditions of service. There was evidence to demonstrate adverse effects on them personally and to their social life outside of school which led many to question how they would sustain themselves physically and mentally as they aged.

The conclusion reached is that headship is unrelenting in terms of the emotional and physical demands it makes as the job becomes all encompassing, generally exceeds the boundaries of the contracted time and frequently invades personal and family life. Government commissioned research into teacher workload in the early part of this new century showed headteachers not only to commonly work more hours per year on average than managers and professionals in other occupations, but also to have a more consistent commitment to the job throughout the year. Managers and professionals in other occupations typically did not work in periods of the year designated as holidays, whereas headteachers not only work around 60 hours per week during term-time, but also for some 130 hours per year on average during holiday periods (Pricewaterhouse Coopers, 2001). The final picture drawn from the government sponsored teacher workload study, and the data gathered through this study, is that headteachers perceive and enact the job as a year-round commitment.

The fact that until recently there was no shortage of applicants for headship is tribute to the resourcefulness and resilience of previous generations. Things are different now and as I write the newspapers are full of stories about an alarming shortage of headteachers, especially in the major cities. Whilst it is true that anyone switching from one job to another is going to experience gains and losses when making the transition, it is assumed that at this point you have taken the decision to make the transition to your first headship because you perceive the gains to outweigh the losses. An interesting way to consider that balance is to employ the model developed by Kelly (1980) as part of a doctoral thesis. Kelly's model employs a quadrant that allows you to compare the gains and losses accumulated through attachment to the new job and detachment from your previous employment. The Gains, Losses, Attachment, Detachment (GLAD) model has been applied to headship in Scotland by researchers who established that for those headteachers investigated the difference between gains and losses was marginal, at least on the surface (see Table 6.1).

Numerically there were nearly twice as many losses as gains for the new Scottish headteachers, although clearly some form of weighting has to be applied to each element before final judgement should be made. Effectively these headteachers had made the decision that they perceived the benefits of moving to a new job to be greater than staying where they were, although in a surprising number of cases increased salary was not a major motivating factor. In fact, there was a clear relationship between the perception of gains and the motivating factors identified in Herzberg's Two Factor Theory of motivation.

Herzberg (1966) established that a sense of achievement, recognition of a person's contribution to the organization, job interest, responsibility and the prospect of advancement were much more significant to managers than what he called the 'hygiene factors' of company policy and administration; the quality of supervision; relations with supervisors, subordinates and colleagues and the quality of social life at work; the total rewards package, such as salary and pension; a person's position or rank in relation to others; job security; the effect of a person's work on family life, for example stress and unsocial hours; and the working conditions. Here you can see clear evidence of these hygiene factors in the losses quoted by the Scottish headteachers. You may care to do your own GLAD analysis as you approach and enter your first headship.

Table 6.1 The GLAD model of career transition applied to headship

	Attachment	Detachment
Gains/Benefits	*School development:* • seeing planned developments take place and having control over the direction of the school; • being able to encourage staff development and professionalism; • being in charge, having financial control and enabling things to happen. *Personal development:* • new things to learn and master and involvement in a wider professional world. *Relationships:* • support received from staff.	*The frustration of:* • working to someone else's agenda; • wanting to change things but having to be at the top to be able to do that; • under-using strengths.
Losses	*Headship burdens:* • the amount of paperwork and bureaucracy; • being overburdened and stressed; • the sense of accountability; • dealing with difficult staff; • greater financial responsibility. *Quality of life effects:* • lack of time for self and family. *Relationship effects:* lack/loss of closeness with staff; lack/loss of contact with pupils; • sense of isolation. *Personal/professional effects:* • lack of time for own professional growth; • salary increased little from previous salary as a deputy; • want to get it right, but fear might not.	• the loss of friendships with and support from previous colleagues and association with pupils; • the sense of competence provided by the 'known'.

Source: Adapted from Draper and McMichael (1998)

Seeking Support in the Early Stages

At point of entry you will need information, advice and guidance with the proportion of each of those elements being contingent on the circumstances you find. Information about systems and processes is usually relatively easy to find as the incumbent members of that school community are generally keen to maintain the status quo and are thus happy to provide you with it. The funding agency that is your employer typically will also seek validation of their current mode of operation and will probably offer induction opportunities that will allow you to familiarize yourself with the personnel and routines that have been established. Sadly, and as has been shown earlier in this book, such induction processes are often either too expensive or too compact to actually help new members come to terms with those potential support mechanisms. The usual consequence is that you are left to find out for yourself and achieve understanding through a process akin to osmosis, although it is more likely to be one of immersion. The thoughts of Dominique, a newly appointed primary headteacher, are illustrative of such feelings:

> For the first couple of terms I really felt that I wasn't me. I was somebody else who was being forced to take a part in a play where I didn't have the script.

Taking control does not come easily to most newly appointed headteachers unless you have been appointed with a clear mandate for effecting change or you have well-founded confidence in your ability. Information offered freely in the early stages needs to be processed carefully, therefore, in order that your beliefs and values are not challenged unfairly or to ensure that your idealism is not shattered unreasonably. Here is where guidance and advice become important. Guidance is central to understanding and operating existing systems and processes, whilst advice allows for informed choices to be made.

The principal sources of guidance are commonly found through coaching, networking and employers. Networking with other key members of the school system is usually the best solution when seeking guidance, as employers and government agencies may have alternative agendas to your personal aspirations. Generally networking will mean establishing and sustaining contact with colleagues in similar or related positions in other schools, as well as working closely with key people within your own school community. A headteacher new to a diocese, for example, would do well to attend formal and informal meetings with their peers. Similarly, the newly appointed headteacher of an independent school would do well to join the local or regional meetings of their colleagues.

The key skill here is to recognize the kinship to be found among headteachers, even where they may be in direct market competition with their peers, as they are the only other people who have some real understanding of the job, of the challenges and of the dissonance of decisions. That does not mean you have to rely exclusively on other headteachers for sensible guidance, but it does mean you should look in that direction as a rule of thumb when seeking guidance on current systems and processes. Other sources of guidance are the officers and advisers who work for your employer who, in some instances, have a direct responsibility for providing you with support on an ongoing basis.

Coaching can be either formal or informal, covering a range of activities from the mastery of simple skills to providing support for the implementation or development of complex management systems. Typically coaching is about the adoption of existing systems or processes, rather than determining which actions to take. When you reach the point where you are making decisions about what to do, your support mechanism needs to be one of advice. You must recognize that the quality of advice on offer to newly appointed headteachers is varied, ranging from that focused by political imperatives through to that which supports free choice. Again, you should make the decision of how you filter that advice when searching for solutions in the same way as you process the information and guidance available to you. Finding sources of non-judgemental advice is one of the key elements needed to make the early stages of a new headship successful.

As was shown in Chapter 2, most headteachers have recommended finding mentors who can help them in this way. That earlier discussion demonstrated that the route to personal effectiveness passes from reflection to emotional intelligence, so early on it would be useful to have another person to assist with that reflection. This is the friend or colleague with whom ideas can be bounced around, where possible solutions can be explored without fear. A major weakness in our society, however, is that we prefer people, especially those who are 'in charge', only to speak when they have fully formed ideas. Thinking aloud often leads to ridicule which can, in turn, suppress potential initiative and imaginative responses. Having a friend or colleague (or indeed several of the same) with whom you can explore possible solutions to challenges and dilemmas, therefore, is extremely worthwhile. Knowing you can trust such people is priceless.

Being an effective mentor is more likely to result from training than natural development. Research into the national Headteacher Mentoring Scheme that ran in England during the early 1990s showed, for example, not only the value of training mentors who could act in a multi-faceted way, but also demonstrated the benefits of training partners in the mentoring relationship conjointly. Subsequently successful relationships were more likely to be a partnership, based on mutual respect, than merely a pairing of a seasoned and new practitioner. Furthermore, the relationship was shown to be mutually beneficial, with the mentors reporting self-development as an outcome of their experiences (Bolam et al., 1993).

You will almost certainly be required to pay for most support services, especially those delivered at an individual level. This should be seen as a good thing as payment will put relationships on a more professional footing than those which are ad hoc or informal. Some employer costs for such support may not be obvious as school income is often 'top-sliced' to pay for these services although, in fairness, most employers now publish service level agreements that specify what you will get for that money. Your job, of course, is to ensure you get value for money. In some instances you may be able to utilise additional employer or grant funding to pay for training, coaching or mentoring services. Funding for such relationships has existed in the maintained sector for first-time headteachers within the

HEADLAMP and HIP schemes in England, for example, although is too early to say how the revamped NCSL programme for Entry to Headship will allow for such use of funds when it commences in 2006.

The major problem in gaining support at this critical time is that systems are not always geared to meeting the problems you are likely to encounter in your personal environment. Most employers, for example, will seek to move you into their existing structures and processes before you have time to take stock of the significance of some elements of the induction process on offer. Similarly for first-time headteachers there is a tendency for personal needs identification and analysis processes to be offered too soon. My research shows that the vast majority of incoming headteachers do not know what their needs are until they have passed through the Entry and Encounter stage of headship which, in some instances, may take more than a year.

This highlights the need for appropriate advice to be available to you in the early stages of your new job and that is why you are recommended to actively seek mentoring relationships which, if operated on the principle of mutual respect, will hasten your development toward becoming a reflective practitioner and one who is emotionally intelligent. From that position you can determine your real needs and identify the combination of training, coaching and advice required to promote your continued development.

Taking Charge and Reshaping

Research demonstrates that most headteachers pass through idealism, uncertainty and adjustment in the first stage of headship for a period of between one and three years (see for example Day and Bakioglu, 1996; Reeves et al., 1998). The next stage is one of taking charge and is a process characterized by movement towards mastery and influence.

> By taking charge, I do not mean just orienting oneself to a new assignment. Taking charge, as I use the term, refers to the process by which a manager establishes mastery and influence in a new assignment. By mastery, I mean acquiring a grounded understanding of the organization, its tasks, people, environment, and problems. By influence, I mean having an impact on the organization, its structure, practices, and performance. (Gabarro, 1987: 6)

The process of reshaping begins once the new leader has developed an understanding of the basic issues and underlying problems, some of which may emerge well before the end of the first year. Reshaping is a time of major change and the busiest time for formal leaders as they seek to exert influence over organizational processes. This is the point where personal expertise should be at its most obvious. As the person selected to be the formal leader of the organization, there is both expectation and licence for you to provide the initiative for change. By dint of its very nature headship is the most central and influential position in the school community and one where the power to change things is most evident. It is at this point, however, that we will see behaviour that will differentiate the effective headteacher from one who has merely accepted the residual power of office.

Firstly, effective headteachers are those who recognize that for decisions taken at senior level, implementation is by those at operational level. The definition of an effective change policy, therefore, is one that will lead to action on the ground that matches the policy objective. Secondly, effective headteachers are those who recognize that the job of leading a school is too big, too varied and too complex for it to be the province of one person. Leadership, therefore, needs to be a collective activity. The two issues come together at the start of the high plains of leadership, with effective head-teachers ensuring they create and sustain a collegial approach to school leadership where individual members of the school community can engage with the identification and implementation of change issues.

At the reshaping stage of your headship you are almost certainly at the point where you can best exhibit your own mastery and influence. You have a grounded understanding of the organization and the personal authority to exhibit influence in more areas of the organization than other individuals or groups. In short, you are competent and confident and may be close to reconciling your substantial self with your situational self. The expertise you bring to the job cannot and should not be denied, however, as this is the time when you make the biggest difference as an individual. Remember, you have been appointed for very good reasons. People obvi-ously believe you have the experience and expertise to lead the school suc-cessfully, so it is a time to believe and trust in yourself. You are a seasoned educationalist and have proven leadership capability, so do not underesti-mate your talents or diffuse them through personal insecurity as your judgement is probably sound. But also you do need to recognize that this is a time when you need to build for the future.

This building for the future involves being strategically focused and expanding leadership capacity within the school community. This is also a period for recognizing that headship is a career and that this school may provide you with the last professional position you will occupy in your working life. Time was when headship was described as cyclical and proba-bly lasting about seven years before disenchantment or itchy feet set in. A typical pattern was for headteachers to establish themselves in the first year, begin a process of change in years two and three, consolidate and perfect those changes in years four to six and then enjoy a seventh year of con-tentment before looking to move on. Obviously this was not a universal truth for there were, and still are, those change experts who can hit and run on a two-year cycle, usually being employed in turn-around situations. Equally there were those who stayed because they enjoyed it and those who stagnated, content to run cruising or strolling schools. For the headteacher going the 'full-term' of seven years, however, there were often options beyond the first headship that provided them with hope for the future.

So much has changed since those earlier days, however, that it is no longer reasonable to think of there being just one cycle of events for a school. Equally, there are few parallel positions to which serving head-teachers can now transfer, mainly because the salary differentials often pre-clude such a move. Moving into advisory work or into higher education, often a career option in the past, nowadays inevitably means a reduced income and possible increased stress.

In all likelihood headship will be a continued pattern of behaviour within the same school community and one that requires a regular reap-praisal of personal and organizational needs. The effective headteacher seeking to remain effective will have to create and sustain organizational structures and processes that accommodate and extend the potential for change in their school. Inevitably this means they will have to develop strategic capability and leadership capacity and these will be the focus of attention within the next chapter when we will explore the issues for con-solidating and extending your headship. At the beginning of the reshaping phase, however, you need to be laying the foundations for that future.

Laying the Foundations for the Future

I have twice now made the point that success in the next stage of your headship is contingent on your ability to lead and manage change in such a way that you build leadership capacity within the school. This is not dogma, based on my ideal of headship in action, but is a pragmatic exer-tion that draws on that core purpose of headship I defined in the opening chapter – to meet the needs of the school community. Needs are qualified wants. Everybody wants something from the school system and one of your principal jobs as headteacher is to elicit, filter and synthesize those wants into a politically acceptable set of needs. To do this effectively you have to establish mechanisms by which all participants in the school community can identify legitimate wants and make a meaningful contribution to deciding which of those wants are genuine needs.

In most instances, but particularly in the state maintained sector, the first step is to create a genuine working partnership with your governing body. Astonishingly this is the first mention of governors since the opening chapter and yet frequently they are the genuine source of power in most schools. In many school systems across the world governance is at a district or regional level, overseeing multiple schools. In England, however, it is virtually universal in that every school, state-maintained or independent, has its own governing body that is largely representative of the community the school serves. Governing bodies, particularly in the state system, are part of the complex system of checks and balances inherent in the administration of public services that reflect the ability of English society to prevent fraud and misuse of resources. For maintained schools the governing body is the legal decision-making arm of the school, responsible for setting policies and monitoring practice.

In many cases this expectation had been realized on a continuum of practice ranging from political interference in the day to day practice of a school by members of the governing body through to a total lack of interest by a group of press-ganged volunteers. At best this range has demonstrated a comforting number of governing bodies taking an active and informed interest in the leadership and management of the school; at worst it has demonstrated too many governing bodies failing to recognize or act on their responsibilities, behaving as a time-consuming, rubber stamp committee wholly dependent on the headteacher. My research has shown that headteacher time spent on governing bodies is more often about breathing life into the edifice rather than working with enthusiastic lay members of the public who act as para-professionals in leading and managing a school. Yet you ignore or abuse your governing body at your peril.

Governing bodies represent the school community you serve and are, in all instances, capable of providing the space in which headteachers can resist or manage change that emanates from those outside the immediate members of the school. Close working relationships, especially with the Chair, are essential, but for the effective headteacher it is critical that the relationship is an alliance. Policy creation and decision making at the school level are fundamentally shaped by political factors that are often outside your immediate control or influence as a headteacher. Central government and employers are key actors in this sense at the macro level, whilst parents and other members of the school community play significant roles at the micro level. Being able to manage those influences requires you, as headteacher, to either resist such powerful forces or align them with your preferred patterns of behaviour. In most circumstances the governing body will be your most important ally, although where the school is in difficulties it may be that you need to look to one of the other key influences for the support that will be critical for your success. Typically, headteachers with the support of their governing body can shape external influences to suit the needs of the school community. In times of continuous pressure for change from central governments such a haven becomes a necessity for headteachers seeking to be the most significant influence in shaping the fortunes of a school.

Having established an effective working relationship with the governing body, the next principal need that must be fulfilled is to establish, sustain and extend the personal relationships with those employed within your school, particularly those at senior level. In the best run organizations there is a high degree of mutual trust between members that is based on experiences of working successfully together. A high degree of commitment to a common cause is evident rather than enrolment to a set of organizational rules, whether explicit or explicit.

As discussed in Chapter 1, Senge (1990) provides a very helpful distinction between the personal states of commitment and enrolment where people are at different stages of compliance with the organizational mores. For an organization to enjoy continued success there must be a set of people in the most influential positions who will work collaboratively to establish, sustain and constantly review core values. They will be the committed ones whose joint influence outweighs that of other members who may be exhibiting alternatively focused views, non-compliance or even apathy. Between the committed and the non-compliant sit those who are happy to go with the flow, either because they are content or because the cost of resistance is too high. This combination of commitment and happy compliance is essential for the organization to achieve the critical mass required to become highly effective in meeting the needs of the community it serves.

In schools this inevitably means establishing good personal relationships with those who are in key positions of authority. As the newly appointed headteacher your task is to establish whether you have the right structure and the people who can operate most effectively in the positions of authority within that structure. By the time you have reached the point of taking hold and reshaping you have almost certainly determined the preferred structure for providing the most appropriate mix of leadership, management and administration required to ensure the needs of your school community will be met. To make the structure work you not only need the right people to fill the key positions of authority, but you will also need to ensure that they have an appropriate level of commitment. This is where the effective headteacher takes on board the canons of the national standards in that they will 'inspire, challenge, motivate and empower others to carry the vision forward' (DfES, 2004). This vision is not a personal one, however, but one forged through collaboration, inclusive of stakeholders' beliefs and values and sustainable within legal and societal expectations. A shared vision means ownership and with that comes commitment.

The concept of ownership is a basic tenet of successful change and is one that requires formal leaders to recognize that change processes should involve the individual in the immediate job situation (Fullan, 1993). In other words, the best way to enhance change is to work closely with those who will operationalize the proposals. Effective headteachers thus seek the opinion and advice of those who work at ground level when defining new policy and practice. Policy, after all, is not that which is espoused by those on high; policy is what you get in practice. Involving those who will be responsible for enacting policy directly by determining it to begin with will considerably enhance the prospects for successful change. Establishing an environment where opinion and experience can inform decision making is a critical skill for aspirant effective headteachers.

A second order, but still vital, skill is to manage the internal conversation in concert with internal and external pressures. Undoubtedly this is a high-order skill and is one contingent on your ability to create a working environment where it is realized that consultation is not the same as democracy. This realization takes us straight back to one of the basic requirements for effective headteachers; to recognize their personal accountability. When consulting with organizational members you need to be doing so within the political frame of reference provided by legitimate national, local and organizational mores. Undoubtedly this will mean, on occasion, that you will disappoint some organizational members who might expect their views not only to be heard but also to be acted upon. The inevitability of that outcome means you need some strategies to deal with that disappointment in order that potential contributors to decision making are not dissuaded unduly from making future contributions because of your rejection of their advice and guidance.

In part the resolution of this challenge is in establishing an environment of trust and in part down to effective communication. Trust grows from engagement in successful experiences, whilst effective communication grows from honesty. As demonstrated above you are bound within the system by legal and societal expectations and within the organization by overt beliefs and values. If an outcome cannot be accommodated within those parameters some potential choices will have to be rejected. One of the central arts of effective headship is to be able to explain and justify such decisions.

Stemming from the dilemma of seeking opinion and advice, but not acting upon it, is the establishment of trust. In order to be effective as a formal leader and to build the capacity to become a high performing school, you need to spread the load and widen the thinking. Spreading the load without widening the thinking is a management response to a dynamic situation and one doomed to failure. Creating leadership capacity means taking risks and placing faith in others to make decisions and to decide on action within an organizational ethos built on a shared values set. Allowing others to interpret and enact those values means you can expect some outcomes that would not have happened if you had limited the decision-making process to yourself or a few senior colleagues. Some of those outcomes might be better than your original expectations whilst some might be worse. All devolution of decision making comes with a risk, therefore, which you need to evaluate before granting permission or encouraging such behaviour. Given your level of personal accountability as a headteacher you might want to put some limits on decision making by others.

A general rule of thumb to employ here is to look at the consequences and then work out which is the worst possible outcome and ask yourself the question "can I live with it?" If you can, then take the risk. If you can't tolerate the worst possible scenario, don't take the risk. Remember, however, that excellence is never achieved without risk. In this case you are seeking to enhance the leadership capacity within your school by giving people permission to fail and as Einstein said "show me someone who hasn't failed and I will show you someone who has learned nothing." Developing leadership capacity is about individuals learning how to take decisions and actions and that will mean some mistakes and failures are inevitable. The trick here is to establish a learning environment for your colleagues that allows for mistakes and failures, but one based on the simple premise that the same mistake should never be repeated!

Towards Consolidation and Extension

Having completed the Entry and Encounter stage and begun the process of Taking Hold and Reshaping, the emphasis now of effective headteacher behaviour is to lay the foundations for the future. Successful completion of this stage will allow you to lead and manage change successfully and to build leadership capacity that will spread the load and widen the thinking. From that position you can engage with the next steps in headship – to consolidate and extend – but that is the focus of the next chapter.

7 | Consolidation and extension

The arguments and logic presented in the previous chapters should mean that by now you have reached the point of headship where you can begin to make a real difference in the long term. You have successfully managed the personal, organizational and occupational transition to headship and now not only feel confident and competent, but are ready to become strategic and to enter the high plains of school leadership. In short, you stand on the threshold of being an effective headteacher. This the point where you become strategic.

Strategic Leadership

There is a myriad range of texts available that tell you *how* to become strategic. This section will focus, however, on *what* to be strategic about. Strategy, in its dictionary definition, is the art and science of employing resources to carry out agreed policies. The *art* of being strategic lies in your ability to manage the multiple variables and influences that exist within and around the complex social system of a school. The *science* of being strategic is to make effective use of the tools available to you to make informed choices and to sustain the intentions of your school community. This activity is governed to a large extent by the changing nature of the macro society in which your school is situated and success is defined by your ability to understand the ebb and flow of such externally driven changes in order to inform decision making that will enhance your school's current and future existence. The strategically focused school, therefore, is one that can sustain or amend its core principles in the face of that external change over which it has little control and influence. Consequently, *what* to be strategic about remains the key issue.

Schools are organizational constructs that basically exist to serve the needs of society and formal education is required of young people in most countries across the world in order to prepare them for their adult existence. Compulsory education in England suffers from a lack of declared intent, as described in Chapter 3, and has a wide range of acceptable provision. Consequently the core purpose of compulsory education is obfuscated both through the activities of various interest groups who are competing for validity and by a range of provision that meets the only declared legal aim – to educate children between the ages of five and sixteen years in a manner commensurate with their age and ability.

The most dominant agency in determining acceptable educational provision in England has been central government which has enacted its power through legal, financial and rhetorical means. The basic component of compulsory education has been the establishment of state-maintained schools which now cater for over 90 per cent of children in England. Such schools exist, it has been argued for decades, for four key purposes: to provide custodial care for vulnerable children; to provide an agency that can act in the best interests of society in general; to provide a means by which we can differentiate between children as to their abilities and capabilities; and, finally, to transmit knowledge which will help and guide them into adult life (see for example Reimer, 1971). Depending on your political perspective, schools can thus be perceived as either socially inclusive or divisive as they seek to satisfy the range of stakeholders to whom they are accountable, but particularly the needs of central government.

A Post-Welfare State

The initial driving force behind the development of this school system in England was the principle of social welfare, an approach that was symptomatic of most legislation in the immediate aftermath of the Second World War. The rebuilding of the nation's economy in the post-1945 period saw greater governmental intervention into the lives of the general population, including the provision of the National Health Service and an investment into the prevention of disease. A healthy nation, it was believed, would lead to a healthy economy, so money was poured into nutrition and mass immunisation in addition to providing better medical care. Schools provided a very effective mechanism for ensuring the welfare of children and it was common practice for a child to be supported in their physical health and growth by school as much as by family. Milk and nutritional supplements were provided on a daily basis, school meal services were established, children were inoculated and their health monitored by government agencies.

Developing the cognitive capability of the school population followed in due course, as less emphasis was placed on selection through the 1960s and more effort was directed toward child-centred education in primary schools and toward comprehensive education in secondary schools. By the early 1970s compulsory education had been extended to the age of sixteen years and all children had access to a broad curriculum. State-maintained schools thus largely attempted to replicate or extend the tasks formerly undertaken by the family and the local community.

Government emphasis shifted during the 1970s, however, from a philosophy of provision to one of accountability. The urgency to build and equip sufficient schools to cater for the population explosion of the 1950s – a consequence of the post-war 'baby boom' – was replaced by a demand for public accountability. Driven mainly by right-wing critics of social reform, successive governments sought to tie education more closely to the economy. Investment in schools had to be matched by enhanced performance, particularly that which could be clearly demonstrated through student attainment on standard tests.

By the late 1980s state-maintained schools in England were operating in a quasi market, in competition for resources, and being judged largely by the aggregated scores of their children on national measures of attainment. A national framework of curriculum and assessment was sustained through external inspection by government agencies towards the end of the century, with these factors providing the most dominant features of school organization and management. Somewhere in this maelstrom of activity lurked children's education and an emergent discourse about the appropriateness of the school system that had evolved as a result of continued government activity.

Building on the four elements of schooling outlined above, Bottery (1992, 2000), has determined different emphases for schooling that provide a lens by which you can define the core purpose of your school. Schools, he suggests, have competing purposes. They can provide a vehicle for the continuation of traditional social systems or they can be used as a means of determining new social structures. Schools can then either be perceived as systems for feeding and sustaining the national economy or for providing a learner-centred environment geared to individual need. Clearly, all four elements can be seen in any school with different levels of importance being given to each element by the members of the school community. The best managed schools are those where there is clear evidence of a dominant element; the most effective schools are those where the dominant element is chosen in relation to the needs of the school community. It is at this point that I declare a clear bias in my view of which of these elements should be dominant – the creation of a learner-centred environment.

Learner-Centred Leadership

Most studies of school effectiveness and school improvement demonstrate that student attainment on standard tests can be considerably enhanced through a close attention to individual performance. Critics of the school effectiveness movement frequently point out that the school system that has evolved as a consequence of higher accountability is inequitable, however, with little change evident in life chances for the most disadvantaged. Nevertheless, central governments continue to invest heavily in improvement programmes and initiatives designed to raise standards, commonly interpreted to mean higher scores on standard tests. Irrespective of the positions adopted by the opposing ideological camps, the truth is to be found in individual student experiences of schooling and, as the headteacher, you have an obligation to examine those experiences from a moral perspective. Becoming an effective headteacher requires you to evaluate the student-focused systems and processes within your school and to initiate decisions regarding their experiences that are morally acceptable to other stakeholders in the school community as well as yourself.

A learner-centred approach to formal education is now offered as a panacea by all participants in the debate about school improvement, although often for different reasons. For those involved in school effectiveness research there is the realization that school processes now need to have a closer attention to individual learning needs than the aggregated approaches used in the early stages of the school improvement movement. In 1998, for example, we saw the introduction in England of the National Literacy Strategy in primary schools, together with a strong recommendation to adopt the 'Literacy Hour'. It was not long before innovative schools and teachers began to adapt the strategy to suit local needs, however, a process of virtual subversion that has now become common practice. Similar adaptations have been made to other global initiatives to make them more focused on individual needs with those innovators often being held up subsequently as exemplars of good practice.

Partly this acceptance of adaptation is because substantial and lasting improvements have been demonstrated by those pioneers, although it is equally true that it is not entirely possible to police the school system to the extent where compliance is guaranteed! Nevertheless, there is a growing realization that the initial reforms and initiatives have run their course in terms of effecting global performance. Student performance at a national level has reached a plateau and further improvement will only be achieved through the enactment of individual response to specific situations. No longer will there be a 'one size fits all' approach and local discretion is not only tolerated, but is encouraged.

Opponents of the school effectiveness movement have always mounted their challenge on a broader stage than student performance on standard tests, however, and have presented arguments based on critical social theory. Central to their concerns is the nature of the curriculum which, in the maintained sector, they consider as having a heavy emphasis on academic and cognitive outcomes at the expense of developing social skills. To be a successful adult, they argue, you need not only to develop a number of personal and social skills in addition to academic attainment, but you must also experience life first-hand and develop some aesthetic appreciation. The acquisition of a knowledge-based curriculum is inadequate preparation for adult life, they argue, whereas the development of skills, particularly learning how to learn, is a more fundamental basis for an effective school experience. In this context an appropriate body of knowledge is not pre-defined, as the active learner will locate relevant knowledge at the time it is needed.

Both views coalesce under the principle of learner-centred education. So, whether it is your intention to improve results, to improve life chances or to aim for both approaches, the model of learner-centred leadership is central to this improvement. Schools capable of diagnosing and responding to individual learning needs and developing curricula that support student development in their current and future environments will be the ones that can truly be called 'effective'. The role of the headteacher in such schools is one of learner-centred leadership at the strategic level for which they will need to develop knowledge, skills and capabilities that support and extend related activities to be undertaken, principally, by others. Those people also need to become leaders of learning and to recognize that their key sphere of leadership activity in that mode is as a facilitator, for this is the domain of second order influence. Research in the field has demonstrated that to be effective in creating and sustaining a successful learning environment you will need advanced knowledge in curriculum and pedagogy and in student and adult learning. You will also need skills in change management, group dynamics, interpersonal relationships and communication and, personally, you will require high levels of energy, resilience, determination, empathy and optimism (see for example Duke, 1987; Leithwood et al., 2004).

Leading Learning

Effective leaders of learning have an understanding of curriculum design, something that would have been seen as second nature in the previous generation. Unfortunately that knowledge base and accompanying skills, so prevalent in the 1970s, have virtually disappeared as the national curriculum and its attendant assessment regime have taken increasing hold over school provision. If the quest is to create effective learning environments within schools then the next generation of headteachers will need to build their capability to design and implement curriculum models that match the needs of their school community.

Take, for example, the case of one school in a community where the traditional industry has been in terminal decline for the two previous generations, but the future lies in a field where there is no resident knowledge or skills –

in this case, fishing is to be replaced by digital media as the mainstay of the local economy. Schoolchildren in this community will need to be offered a curriculum that builds thinking and practical skills, uses their imagination and engages them in activities that are alien to the parental view of education, with all of this to be conducted against a backdrop of chronic unemployment. Clearly, a subject-based curriculum created around the transmission of traditional knowledge is inappropriate for these students who will need an interactive, electronically-based learning environment if they are to be able to contribute to future wealth creation in their community. Designing and implementing such a curriculum will take all the personal qualities outlined above, especially determination, optimism and resilience!

Effective learning environments need practitioners who have high levels of pedagogical skills and an understanding of student learning. Pedagogy is the art, science and flair of teaching, demonstrated in practice by a teacher's ability to diagnose and respond appropriately to learning needs. As headteacher you will not only personally need this knowledge, but you will also have to help the other adults who work in the school to achieve a level of understanding appropriate to their job responsibilities. Inevitably this will mean you need to sustain a programme of continuous staff development and for that you will need an understanding of adult learning.

The inevitability of this expectation lies, once again, in the effects of a national curriculum and assessment processes which have influenced teacher education to the point where large numbers of the workforce do not have a grasp of the fundamental and applied psychological constructs of learning that will allow them to provide a differentiated programme in the quest to match student learning needs. The development of that knowledge is now an in-service activity, where in previous generations it may have been pre-service. The success of such a development programme will be based on your capability to lead change, to have good communication and interpersonal skills and to understand group dynamics, particularly team-building.

This knowledge and understanding of curriculum, pedagogy and learning are brought together and deployed by the learning-centred leader in a pattern of modelling, monitoring and dialogue (Southworth, 2002). The larger the school, the fewer opportunities there will be for headteachers to become directly involved with those who are first order practitioners. Schools now typically employ larger numbers of staff, with more adults today working as para-professionals than in previous generations.

Headteachers are now more likely to have to exert influence over the quality of student learning than become directly involved, with that influence being demonstrated in the first instance by modelling. The behaviour of headteachers influences the behaviour of others and those who demonstrate that all key decisions are based on the needs of students will be modelling the basis of an effective learning environment. This aim to model appropriate behaviour will be further influenced if the headteacher can also be shown to be a learner in their own right and actively pursuing their own professional development.

Monitoring has to move beyond a model of accountability and into the realm of reflective discourse, hence the importance of dialogue in learner-centred leadership. Effective schools are characterized by an increased discussion of student learning rather than managerial or behavioural issues. Monitoring based on the principle of shared, reflective learning is the aim and an effective headteacher establishes an environment of mutual trust where this can happen. What quickly becomes apparent is that building an effective learning environment is beyond the efforts of one person alone, so the key task of headship is to build the capability of others to exhibit learner-centred leadership at all levels of a school.

Building Leadership Capacity

Bearing in mind that the working definition of leadership used in this book is based on the ability and opportunity to choose which actions to take, a highly effective school is one where appropriate decisions are taken at all levels of the organization. Guidance for these comes from a shared and explicit values base, as discussed in Chapter 3. To be successful in meeting the learning needs of the students in your school, you will need to encourage and support individuals as they make choices which correspond to these values and to their level of authority. Decisions that lead to effective change, as demonstrated in the previous chapter, are best made at the operational level. Consequently you need to create a structure and an environment that will allow for increased decision making throughout the school. These are the active ingredients of building leadership capacity in your quest to be learner-centred.

Structurally you need to liberate the leadership potential within your school by limiting the direct involvement of the senior leadership team in operational decisions. An effective working model is provided by Carmichael (cited in Sawatzki, 1997: 151) which demonstrates the shift from a hierarchical, bureaucratic model to a new arrangement featuring a very lean strategic core 'steering' a system of self-managing work teams (see Figure 7.1).

Effectively, the school becomes a collection of work units each of which has the authority to take the action that is appropriate to student needs and which corresponds to the shared and explicit values base of the school. The task of the headteacher and the senior leadership team is to provide strategic direction and to monitor activity to see that it is mutually supportive and accords to the declared and implicit intentions of the school community.

The environment that will support this transition to shared leadership is, ultimately, one of risk. Centralized decision making and high profile management prevent failure, but they do not lead to excellence. High performance and excellence come from risk which means, on occasions, that there will be failures. Your mission as headteacher, as stated repeatedly throughout this book, is to evaluate the potential risk and determine whether you can live with the consequences of any such failure. The devolution of decision making, therefore, needs to be balanced against the potential cost of failure. Without risk, however, decisions will be constrained by the limits both of your ability and your stamina. The creation of a learner-centred school cannot be achieved by singular effort, so investment in the leadership development of others is critical to your effectiveness as headteacher.

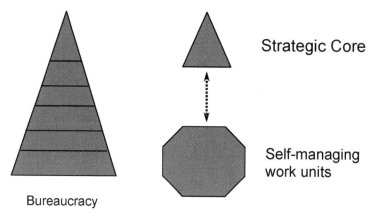

Figure 7.1 A system of self-managing work teams
Source: Sawatzi (1997)

The transition to shared leadership is not a single step, however, as people have to learn how to be free as much as a domestically bred wild animal needs to learn how to live on its own. Raising a fox cub from birth and then successfully releasing it into the wild, for example, requires something more than opening the door to freedom. Similarly staff in schools will need to be engaged in various levels of decision-making environments before being given the liberty to choose without the direct involvement of the headteacher and other members of the senior leadership team. Work on strategies for leadership in team-based organizations by Wilson et al. (1994) is particularly helpful here (see Figure 7.2). This five-level model demonstrates the need to move through various models of decision making before arriving at a desirable state of high empowerment. Your school's context will determine the level at which you can safely devolve decision making and by this stage of your headship you should be able to evaluate how quickly you are likely to be able to move to this final tier where leadership is shared widely and decisions best reflect the needs of the school community.

Central to this organization model are the principles that underpin successful teams. Once again, there are many suitable books available to help you identify potential teams and develop their capacity to be effective (see for example Katzenbach and Smith, 1994), so I will focus on just a few key elements of teamwork at this juncture.

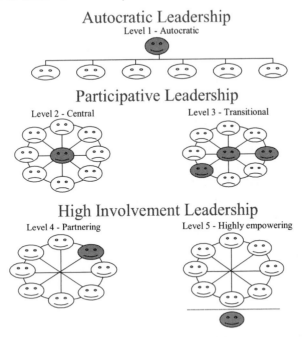

Figure 7.2 Strategies for leadership in team-based organizations
Source: Wilson et al. (1994)

The wisdom of teams is that the collective outcomes will be greater than the individual inputs. We all know this and spend a great deal of our working lives encouraging the formation of teams in the hope that we can appreciate the fruits of their successful labour. The essence of successful teams, however, is people's willingness to give of themselves with no guarantee of getting anything back. If that willingness is not evident then there is no prospect of people becoming a team, as individual members will spend most of their energy making sure their personal circumstances are not affected by the efforts of the group.

It is critical to your development as a headteacher that you not only recognize where these prospects are not good, but also that you are strong enough to avoid continuing your support for such an ambition where it would clearly be a counter-productive use of time and energy. Working groups are still more effective than pseudo teams and although they may not have achieved the ideal state of a team, these can still operate at high levels without the relinquishing of individual political objectives.

By this stage of your headship you should be in a position, therefore, where you can see how much work is needed to move your school into high levels of performance and how long it will be until you have reached that plateau in the high plains of leadership. You will know when you have arrived as you will tend to be less visible and central to the daily work of the school. You are still vital to the organization in the same way, as previously stated in Chapter 1, that oil is to a working engine in that the system will keep running very smoothly for some considerable time without your intervention, although it will eventually seize up. When the school is running that well, this is the point where you need to be asking yourself "what next?"

Reviewing and Re-shaping Headship

A number of options are beginning to emerge for serving headteachers with the result that they can enjoy a fitting career structure and can engage in work opportunities that lift them above the plateau. This is encouraging, as by the end of the last century it was beginning to look as if headteachers were to be consigned to a singular existence at school where the inevitability of disenchantment loomed large. In the early days of the new millennium new opportunities are appearing for the committed professional, however, that can move them beyond the option of taking a second or multiple headship positions.

The career choice of a different headship is, of course, an entirely viable and laudable option, but the chance to engage in a range of activities that extends the professional experience of serving headteachers is a welcome addition to those who have completed the first cycle of headship and have arrived at the plateau. The options currently include personal in-service development programmes such as the Leadership Programme for Serving Headteachers (LPSH), or the adoption of a number of further responsibilities, such as executive headship, becoming a consultant, coach, mentor or trainer on local and/or national programmes for the development of headteachers and senior staff in schools, or an involvement in pre-service or in-service teacher education with Higher Education Institutions (HEIs). All such opportunities provide that additional edge to the job that effective headteachers appear to need if they are to retain their dynamism.

The Leadership Programme for Serving Headteachers

The LPSH is the only nationally sponsored programme of in-service education for serving headteachers in England. Funded by the NCSL, this programme is offered to headteachers who have been in post for at least three years and are seeking to develop their capacity to lead school improvement. Initially devised and offered by the TTA in 1998, it firstly provides the participant with an invaluable opportunity to evaluate their relationships and impact with their school community through the administration of a questionnaire to key members of the school's staff and governing body. Through analysis of these multiple views the headteacher is provided with a measure of the gap between their own perceptions of leadership performance and the perception of others who are in a direct working relationship with them in the school. This has been welcomed as a powerful learning instrument by the vast majority of the participants in the programme, especially where the feedback has been handled sensitively. Secondly, the programme seeks to enhance participant knowledge and understanding through a carefully planned and theoretically sound residential training session. Almost universally this training has been rated highly by participants as it is led by excellent facilitators and is focused, relevant and contemporary.

There are supplementary benefits from this aspect of the programme, however, that are often undersold in the formal evaluations. By locating these residential training sessions in good quality accommodation the participants feel valued; in giving them licence to be away from school they are provided with an opportunity to reflect on their experiences; and those acts of reflection are not only conducted in the company of fellow headteachers, but are also enhanced by the fact that they are mixing with colleagues from different school systems. The net result is that a participant is provided with an outstanding opportunity to make sense of their professional existence and their contribution toward that world. The programme then provides ongoing support through further analysis, extended feedback, mentoring and coaching according to need and commitment on an individual basis.

This glowing recommendation does not mean to say that the programme is without criticism and I have been numbered among those critics in the past (Male, 2000). One major concern, in this case expressed in the formal review of the programme conducted for the NCSL in 2001, was that it was seen as an end point to headteacher development when it should really only be seen as a beginning for the career headteacher (Collarbone, 2001). My principal concerns were two-fold, in that the focus of the programme was heavily geared toward an abstract model of schooling rather than the reality faced by most participants and that the models on which serving headteachers were expected to develop their own construction of leadership were heavily biased towards the experiences of men only. A robust defence of my latter concern was conducted immediately by one of my academic colleagues who claimed that the programme in action was anything but androcentric, an assessment I am happy to concede is probably accurate now, although I was far from convinced at the time as there was little evidence of that aim being reflected in the materials recommended for further professional development.

Yet my fundamental concern remains in that both the feedback and focus of the training are geared toward a model of schooling that is idealistic rather than realistic. As I have argued in earlier chapters, measures of effectiveness are created in regard to the unique circumstances of the school community and are not universal to the national system. Programmes of school improvement are thus specifically rather than generically derived and my argument with the LPSH programme is that it is based largely on an idealistic, abstract notion of school effectiveness. Its usefulness to all participants is contingent, therefore, on their ability to utilise the components in regard to their individual circumstances. As with all headship decisions the application of new knowledge needs to be set against your personal value sets and the needs of your school community, but by this stage of the book you should already know this!

Executive Headship

The term 'Executive Headteacher' has a number of meanings and is one that appears to be gaining currency, often but not wholly associated with federations or the linking of schools. A review of school federations in England for the DfES noted that 'school federation embraces many variants on the concept of inter-school working' (Potter, 2004: 3). Although the DfES funded and approved 35 federations at that time (Department for Education and Skills, 2005) there are many more examples of federated schools that range between informal partnerships to single multi-site schools, some of which have their origins historically, whilst other informal collaborative arrangements have emerged between maintained schools and schools not maintained by local education authorities such as city technology colleges, academies and independent schools (and further education institutions). The essential difference is one of school governance, with 'hard' federations being those that have a common governing body, whether that is a single body or a joint committee representing each school. The DfES determined that federations can thus be defined in two ways:

- The definition as invoked in the 2002 Education Act which allows for the creation of a single governing body or a joint governing body committee across two or more schools from September 2003 onwards.
- A group of schools with a formal (this is to say written) agreement to work together to raise standards, promote inclusion, find new ways of approaching teaching and learning and build capacity between schools in a coherent manner. This will be brought about in part through structural changes in leadership and management, in many instances through making use of the joint governance arrangements invoked in the 2002 Education Act.

These types of federations thus sit at the hard end of a whole spectrum of collaborative arrangements, although the DfES indicates a keenness to promote collaboration at all levels in the understanding that schools need to take a measured and staged approach to cooperation and collaboration to ensure long-term impact and success.

In general, therefore, federations can be separated into either self-deter-mined federations or support federations. Self-determined federations are based upon voluntary collaboration in which schools share goals and the perception that joint working facilitates the achievement of these goals (Bentley and Wilsden, 2003). Support federations are characterized by an association between a successful school and one or more struggling schools. Such federations may or may not be permanent arrangements and are often brokered by a local authority, the DfES or both of these.

Irrespective of the nature of the federation, a career opportunity is emerg-ing for the lead headteacher in these collaborative ventures with the post usually being referred to as 'Executive Headteacher'. To formally have this title within the maintained schools sector, however, the postholder would have to be awarded a separate contract, negotiated between the governing body and the local authority. Research conducted for the DfES identified arrangements for executive headship as comprising:

- running two schools as one under a single head, which may or may not be a permanent arrangement;
- the development of a family of schools, each with its own headteacher, under the oversight of an executive head, which is a permanent arrange-ment (a hard federation);
- the cloning of excellent schools, which is a permanent arrangement;
- satellite schools: extensive support including key staff is provided by the lead partner for a limited period whilst the partner school retains auton-omy, including after the contract comes to an end.

(Potter, 2004: 6–7)

In a small-scale study undertaken in England by the NCSL in late 2004 with headteachers from secondary and special schools who matched this description, participants taking on the post saw it as one way of redefining the traditional career path of heads and providing a means of meeting new challenges to take them beyond the demands of their own school. Whilst some felt the individual or lead school's financial rewards to be important, their motivation was more about staying 'at the cutting edge' and refresh-ing the lead school and self with new experiences (Barnes et al., 2005). In short, a way of retaining interest in the headship.

The Headteacher as Consultant, Coach, Mentor or Trainer

The clearest example of this possible route into career extension and devel-opment in England is to be seen in the position of Consultant Leader first devised by the NCSL in 2003. Their development programmes and activi-ties in the area of consultant leadership seek to support senior staff in schools, including headteachers, who have a proven track record of success and thus equip them with the skills necessary to take up the challenge of developing others.

The NCSL development programme for consultant leaders focuses on facilitation and consultancy skills and is firmly rooted in client-centred change. Successful applicants to the programme will be able to demonstrate a close match to the published competencies and, once accepted, will participate in two phases of residential training supplemented by on-line materials that will prepare them to be appointed as Consultant Leaders. Once this happens, there will be opportunities to work on a number of NCSL-sponsored activities as consultant, coach, mentor or trainer.

There is potential for great variation when lending your experience, knowledge and skill to the development of others in this manner. There are qualitatively different experiences between coaching and mentoring, for example, and both can be mutually rewarding to the facilitator and those they seek to support. Similar differences can be seen between acting as a consultant and as a trainer, with all roles carrying endless potential for personal interest and growth as well as providing essential support of others. In addition to the personal development that will emanate from facilitating the development of others, there is also the chance for income to be generated which could offset the costs to the school of releasing the headteacher for such duties.

The strength of the NCSL in that regard is the funding they hold for such activities, although the promotion and support for such activities are neither confined to these nor a prerequisite, as you may decide to work in this way for professional or altruistic reasons. All such roles provide the potential for career extension, however, and that is the clear message to emerge from engaging in such activities irrespective of the funding sources.

Teacher Education

Changes to the funding mechanisms for initial teacher education (ITE) and in-service education and training (INSET) in England at the end of the last century have been instrumental in moving resources to schools at the expense of Higher Education. This factor, coupled with fundamental shifts in the concepts of teacher education, has opened up a range of opportunities for headteachers to develop their personal and career interests in conjunction with HEIs.

ITE is now heavily dependent on school-based experience that is supported from within a school at least as much as from the HEI. In addition to the vital mentoring role, often undertaken by the classroom-based teacher, schools are also involved in the assessment of students and in the governance and management of the teacher certification process. There are many opportunities, therefore, for headteachers to extend their professional experience along this dimension of teacher education.

Similar opportunities exist for the headteacher who wishes to engage in the determination, management, delivery, and evaluation of in-service activities beyond their own school. These opportunities could exist collectively or individually with other key agencies in the field. In addition to the local authority, these agencies could include national providers in England such as the Training and Development Agency (TDA) and the General Teaching Council (GTC) or more locally based providers including Learning Skills Councils, HEIs and regional consortia. All such agencies require and depend on school-based practitioners to guide and support the in-service activities that follow.

A third, and growing, aspect of headteacher career enhancement and development is as part-time members of course teams in HEIs, particularly for higher degree programmes. With teaching rapidly becoming an all graduate profession on entry, the scope for higher degree programmes has both broadened and narrowed at the same time. Masters programmes are often now of less significance to prospective headteachers, as the pre-service national programmes such as the NPQH have become more central to development needs for aspiring school leaders. Nevertheless, the total number of registrations for higher degrees in education-related studies has remained fairly constant for the last thirty years. The pay structure in HE does not make it a financially beneficial full-time career option for most serving headteachers, but the opportunities to become an associate lecturer do exist. Certainly, the degree programmes for which I have responsibility would not be sustainable without the part-time staff I can employ, some of whom are still serving headteachers. The benefits to the university of having a serving headteacher working on the programmes is self evident; the benefits to a headteacher are not so immediately obvious, but those who have become involved generally speak of enjoying the intellectual challenge.

A Final Word

Moving on, moving up or moving out? My feeling is that the demands of headship have changed and that getting to the plateau is a somewhat longer journey than may have been typical in the past. There will come a point, however, when the time to move becomes evident. You will know this point, but don't be surprised if the new job is as demanding as the old one!

For those leaving the profession, I would wish that you do so with fond memories and, hopefully, a feeling that you had not quite finished. As one of the participants to my national survey commented, "this is still a brilliant job despite everything thrown at it." May your experiences lead to the same, happy conclusion. Enjoy.

References

Argyris, C. and Schön, D. (1974) *Theory in Practice: Increasing professional effectiveness*. San Francisco, CA: Jossey-Bass.

Barnes, I., Coleman, A., Creasy, J. and Paterson, F. (2005) *Executive Headship: A study of heads who are leading two or more secondary or special schools*. Nottingham: National College for School Leadership.

Barnett, B. (2001, March) *The Professional Induction of Beginning Principals in Colorado*. Paper presented to the annual meeting of the American Educational Research Association, Seattle, USA.

Bass, B. (ed.) (1981) *Stodgill's Handbook of Leadership*. New York: Free Press.

Becker, H. (1964) 'Personal change in adult life', *Sociometry*, 27 (March): 40–53.

Bentley, T. and Wilsden, J. (eds) (2003) *The Adaptive State*. London: Demos.

Bolam, R. (1997) 'Management development for headteachers: Retrospect and prospect', *Educational Management & Administration*, 25 (3): 265–83.

Bolam, R. (2004) 'Reflections on the NCSL from a historical perspective', *Educational Management Administration & Leadership*, 32 (3): 251–67.

Bolam, R., McMahon, A., Pocklington, K. and Weindling, D. (1993) *National Evaluation of the Headteacher Mentoring Pilot Schemes: A report for the Department for Education*. London: HMSO.

Bottery, M. (1992) *The Ethics of Educational Management*. London: Cassell.

Bottery, M. (2000) *Education, Policy and Ethics*. London: Continuum.

Boyzatsis, R. (1982) *The Competent Manager: A model for effective performance*. New York: John Wiley.

Brezinha, W. (1994) *Socialization and Education: Essays in conceptual criticism*. Westport, CT: Greenwood Press.

Brundrett, M. (2001) 'The development of school leadership programmes in England and the USA: A comparative analysis', *Educational Management & Administration*, 29 (2): 229–45.

Bush, T. (1998) 'The National Professional Qualification for Headship: The key to effective school leadership?', *School Leadership & Management*, 18 (3): 321–23.

Coleman, M. (1996) 'Barriers to career progress for women in education: The perception of female headteachers', *Educational Research*, 38 (3): 317–32.

Coleman, M. (2005) *Gender and Headship in the Twenty-first Century*. Nottingham: National College for School Leadership.

Collarbone, P. (2001) *Leadership Programme for Serving Headteachers: A review*. Nottingham: National College for School Leadership.

Collins, J. (2001) *Good to Great.* London: Random House.

Covey, S. (1992) *The Seven Habits of Highly Effective People.* London: Simon & Schuster.

Crow, G. (2003) *School Leader Preparation: A short review of the knowledge base.* Nottingham: National College for School Leadership.

Culbertson, J. (1988) 'A century's quest for a knowledge base', in S. Boyan and J. Norman (eds), *Handbook of Research: Educational Administration.* New York: Longman.

Daresh, J. (1988) *The pre-service preparation of American educational administrators: Retrospect and prospect.* Paper presented at the Research Meeting of the British Educational Management and Administration Society (BEMAS), Cardiff, Wales, April.

Daresh, J. (1995) *Alternative career formation perspectives: Lessons for educational leadership from law, medicine and training for the priesthood.* Paper presented to the annual meeting of the University Council for Educational Administration, Salt Lake City, USA, October.

Daresh, J. and Male, T. (2000) 'Crossing the border into school leadership: Experiences of newly appointed British headteachers and American principals', *Educational Management & Administration,* 28 (1): 89–101.

Day, C. and Bakioglu, A. (1996) 'Development and disenchantment in the professional lives of headteachers', in I. Goodison and A. Hargreaves (eds), *Teachers' Professional Lives.* London: Falmer.

Deal, T. and Peterson, K. (1999) *Shaping School Culture: The heart of leadership.* San Francisco, CA: Jossey Bass.

Department for Education and Employment (1999) *Quinquennial Review of the Teacher Training Agency.* Annesley: DfEE Publications.

Department of Education and Science (1977) *Ten Good Schools: A secondary school enquiry.* London: HMSO.

Department for Education and Skills (2004) *National Standards for Headteachers.* Annesley: DfES Publications.

Department for Education and Skills (2005) *What are federations?* DfES web-site: www.standards.dfes.gov.uk/federations. Accessed October, 2005.

Donmoyer, R., Imber, M. and Scheurich, J. (1995) (eds) *The Knowledge Base in Educational Administration: Multiple perspectives.* New York: SUNY Press.

Draper, J. and McMichael, P. (1998) 'Making sense of primary headship: The surprises awaiting new heads', *School Leadership & Management,* 18 (2): 197–211.

Duke, D. (1987) *School Leadership and Instructional Improvement.* New York: Random House.

Dunning, G. (1996) 'Management problems for new primary headteachers', *School Organisation,* 16 (1): 111–28.

Dunphy, T. and Scott, C. (2000) *The Competency Profile.* London: Hay McBer.

Durcan, J. (1994) *Leadership: A Question of Culture.* Berkhamstead: Ashridge College.

Earley, P. (1992) *The School Management Competencies Project.* Crawley: School Management South.

Earley, P., Evans, J., Collarbone, P., Gold. A. and Halpin, D. (2002) *Research report 336: Establishing the current state of school leadership in England.* Norwich: HMSO.

Eraut, M. (1994) *Developing Professional Knowledge and Competence.* London: Falmer.

Fullan, M. (1993) *Change Forces*. London: Falmer.

Gabarro, J. (1987) *The Dynamics of Taking Charge*. Boston: Harvard Business School Press.

Gardner, H. (1997) *Extraordinary Minds*. London: Weidenfield & Nicholson.

Greenfield, W. (1977) 'Adminstrative candidacy: A process of new role learning – Part 2', *Journal of Educational Administration*, 15 (2): 170–93.

Greenfield, W. (1985) 'The moral socialization of school administrators: Informal role learning outcomes', *Education Administration Quarterly*, 21 (4): 99–119.

Gronn, P. (1993) Psychobiography on the couch: character, biography and the comparative study of leaders. *Journal of Applied Behavioural Science*, 29 (3): 14–32.

Hay Group (2002) *Breakthrough Leadership that Transforms Schools: An exploratory study*. London: Hay Group Management Ltd.

Herzberg, F. (1966) *Work and the Nature of Man*. New York: Staple Press.

Hobson, A., Brown, E., Ashby, P., Keys, W. and Sharp, C. (2003) *Issues for Early Headship: Problems and support strategies*. Nottingham: National College for School Leadership.

Hodgkinson, C. (1991) *Educational Leadership: The moral art*. Albany, NY: SUNY.

Hofstede, G. (1980) *Culture's Consequences*. Thousand Oaks, CA: Sage.

Hofstede, G. (1994) *Culture and Organisations: Software of the mind*. London: HarperCollins.

Hopkins, D. (2001) *School Improvement for Real*. London: Routledge Falmer.

House of Commons Select Committee on Education and Employment (1998) *Ninth report: The role of headteachers*. London: HMSO.

Howson, J. (2005) *Annual Survey of Senior Staff Appointments in England and Wales*. Oxford: Educational Data Surveys.

Inkeles, A. and Levinson, D. (1969) 'National character: The study of modal personality and sociocultural systems', in G. Lindsey and E. Aronson (eds), *The Handbook of Social Psychology* (4th Edition). Reading, MA: Addison-Wesley.

Jirasinghe, D. and Lyons, G. (1996) *The Competent Head: A job analysis of heads' tasks and personality factors*. London: Falmer.

Jones, G. (1986) 'Socialization tactics, self-efficacy, and newcomers' adjustments to organizations', *Academy of Management Journal*, 29: 262–79.

Joyce, B. and Showers, B. (1988) *Student Achievement through Staff Development*. London: Longman.

Katzenbach, J. and Smith, D. (1994) *The Wisdom of Teams: Creating the high performance organisation*. Singapore: McGraw-Hill.

Kelly, G. (1980) *A Study of the Manager's Orientation towards the Transition from Work to Retirement*. Unpublished PhD Thesis, University of Leeds.

Klemp, G. (1980) *The Assessment of Occupational Competence*. Cited in Boyzatsis (1982) Report to the National Institute of Education, Washington, DC.

Leithwood, K., Begley, P. and Cousins, J. (1994) *Developing Expert Leadership for Future Schools*. London: Falmer.

Leithwood, K., Jantzi, D. and Steinbach, R. (1999) *Changing Leadership for Changing Times*. Buckingham: Open University Press.

Leithwood, K., Seashore-Louis, K., Anderson, S. and Wahlstrom, K. (2004) *How Leadership Influences Student Learning: Review of research*. New York: Wallace Foundation.

Lortie, D. (1975) *Schoolteacher*. Chicago, IL: University of Chicago Press.

Lumby, J. (1995) 'Concepts or competence?', *Education,* 17 November, 7–15.

MacKenzie, R. (2005) *To What Extent Does Second Headship Offer a Way Forward in Meeting the Needs of Continuing Career Development for Secondary School Leaders?* Unpublished MBA dissertation, University of Hull.

Mahony, T. (2004) *Principled Headship: A teacher's guide to the galaxy.* Camarthen: Crown House Publishing.

Male, T. (1996) 'Making time to manage', *Management in Education,* 10 (5): 15–16.

Male, T. (1998) *The impact of national culture on school leadership in England.* Paper presented to the annual meeting of the American Educational Research Association, San Diego, CA, USA, April.

Male, T. (2000) 'LPSH – some comments and observations', *Management in Education,* 14 (2): 6–8.

Male, T. (2001) Is the National Professional Qualification for Headship making a difference? *School Leadership & Management,* 21 (4): 463–77.

Male, T. (2004) *Preparing for and entering headship in England: A study of career transition.* Unpublished PhD Thesis, University of Lincoln.

Male, T. and Male, D. (2001) 'Special school headteachers' perception of role readiness', *European Journal of Special Needs Education,* 16 (2): 149–66.

Male, T. and Merchant, B. (2000) 'Chief executive or lead professional?', in K. Stott and V. Trafford (eds), *Partnerships: Shaping the future of education.* London: Middlesex University Press.

March, J. G. and Olsen, J. P. (1976) *Ambiguity and Choice in Organisations.* Bergen: Bergen Universitetsforlaget.

McClelland. D. (1973) 'Testing for competence rather than for "intelligence"', *American Psychologist,* 28 (1): 1–4.

Merton, R. (1968) *Social Theory and Social Structure* (3rd ed.). New York: Free Press.

Morgan, C., Hall, V. and Mackay, H. (1983) *The Selection of Secondary School Headteachers.* Buckingham: Open University Press.

National College for School Leadership (2004) *The Impact of Participation in the National Professional Qualification for Headship.* Nottingham: National College for School Leadership.

National Policy Board for Educational Administration (1989) *Improving the Preparation of School Administrators: An agenda for reform.* Charlottesville, VA: NPBEA.

Nias, J. (1989) 'Teaching and self', in M. Holly and C. McLoughlin (eds), *Perspectives on Teacher Professional Development.* London: Falmer Press.

Office for Standards in Education (2002) *Leadership and Management Training for Headteachers: Report by HMI.* London: Ofsted Publications.

Office for Standards in Education (2005) *Annual Report of the Chief Inspector of Schools.* London: Ofsted Publications.

Ortiz, F. and Marshall, C. (1988) 'Women in educational administration', in N. Boyan (ed.), *Handbook of Research on Educational Administration.* New York: Longman.

Parkay, F. and Hall, G. (1992) *Becoming a Principal.* Boston, MA: Allyn and Bacon.

Peters, R. S. (ed.) (1976) *The Role of the Head.* London: Routledge & Kegan Paul.

Peters, T. and Waterman, R. (1982) *In Search of Excellence.* London: Harper & Row.

Potter, D. (2004) *School Federation: Research project for Academies Division, Depart-*

ment for Education and Skills. London: Department for Education and Skills.

Pricewaterhouse Coopers (2001) *Teacher Workload Study*. London: Pricewaterhouse Coopers.

Pugh, D. and Hickson, D. (1989) *Writers on Organizations* (4th ed.) Harmondsworth: Penguin.

Reeves, J., Moos, L. and Forrest, J. (1998) 'The school leader's view', in: J. MacBeath (ed.), *Effective School Leadership*. London: Paul Chapman Publishing/Sage.

Reimer, E. (1971) *School is Dead: An essay on alternatives in education*. London: Penguin.

Ribbins, P. (1997) 'Heads on deputy headship: Impossible roles for invisible role holders?', *Educational Management & Administration*, 25 (3): 295–308.

Richards, J. (1997) 'The way we were', *Guardian*, 15 August, 2–3.

Sawatzki, M. (1997) 'Leading and managing staff for high performance', in B. Davies and L. Ellison (eds), *School Leadership for the 21st Century*. London: Routledge.

Schein, E. (1988) 'Organizational socialization and the profession of management', *Sloan Management Review*, 53–65.

Scheurich, J. (1995) 'The knowledge base in educational administration: Postposivitist reflections', in R. Donmoyer, M. Imber and J. Scheurich (eds), *The Knowledge Base in Educational Administration: Multiple perspectives*. New York: SUNY Press.

Schön, D. (1987) *Educating the Reflective Practitioner*. San Francisco, CA: Jossey-Bass.

School Management Task Force (1990) *Developing School Management: The way forward*. London: HMSO.

Senge, P. (1990) *The Fifth Discipline: The art and practice of the learning organization*. New York: Doubleday.

Sergiovanni, T. (1992) *Moral Leadership: Getting to the heart of school improvement*. San Francisco, CA: Jossey-Bass.

Shipton, J. and Male, T. (1998) 'Deputy headteachers and the NPQH', *Management in Education*, 12 (3): 7–9.

Southworth, G. (2000) *School leadership in English schools at the close of the twentieth century: Puzzles, problems and cultural insights*. Paper presented to the annual meeting of the American Education Research Association, New Orleans, USA, April.

Southworth, G. (2002) 'Instructional leadership in schools: Reflections and empirical evidence', *School Leadership & Management*, 22 (1): 73–91.

Southworth, G. (2004) 'A response from the National College for School Leadership', *Educational Management Administration & Leadership*, 32 (3): 339–54.

Spencer, L. and Spencer, S. (1993) *Competence at Work: Models for superior performance*. New York: John Wiley.

Taylor, W. (1968) 'Training the head', in B. Allen (ed.), *Headship in the 1970s*. Oxford: Blackwell.

Teacher Training Agency (1996) *Consultation Paper on Training for Serving Headteachers*. London: Teacher Training Agency.

Teacher Training Agency (1997) *National Standards for Headteachers*. London: Teacher Training Agency.

Teacher Training Agency (1998a) *Leadership Programme for Serving Headteachers: Handbook for participants*. London: Teacher Training Agency.

Teacher Training Agency (1998b) *National Standards for Headteachers.* London: Teacher Training Agency.

Thody, A. (1998) 'Training school principals, educating school governors', *International Journal of Educational Management*, 12 (50): 232–39.

Torrington, D. and Weightman, J. (1989) *The Reality of School Management.* Oxford: Blackwell.

Trompenaars, F. and Hampden-Turner, C. (1997) *Riding the Waves of Culture: Understanding cultural diversity in business.* London: Nicholas Brealey.

Valverde, L. (1980) 'Promotion socialization: The informal process in large urban districts and its adverse effects on non-whites and women', *Journal of Educational Equity and Leadership*, 1: 26–46.

Van Maanen, J. (1978) 'People processing: Major strategies of organizational socialization and their consequences', in U. Paap (ed.), *New Directions in Human Resource Management.* Englewood Cliffs, NJ: Prentice Hall.

Van Maanen, J. and Schein, E. (1978) 'Toward a theory of organization socialization', in B. Staw (ed.), *Research in Organizational Behavior.* Greenwich, CT: JAI Press.

Weaver-Hart, A. (1993) *Principal Succession: Establishing leadership in schools.* Albany, NJ: SUNY Press.

Weindling, D. (2000) *Stages of headship: A longitudinal study of the principalship.* Paper presented at the annual meeting of the American Educational Research Association, New Orleans, USA, April.

Weindling, D. (2003) *Leadership Development in Practice: Trends and innovations.* Nottingham: National College for School Leadership.

Weindling, D. and Earley, P. (1987) *Secondary Headship: The first years.* Windsor: NFER-Nelson.

Weindling, D. and Pocklington, K. (1996) 'Promoting reflection on headship through the mentoring mirror', *Educational Management & Administration*, 24 (2): 175–91.

West-Burnham, J. and O'Sullivan, F. (1998) *Leadership and Professional Development in Schools.* London: Pitman.

Wilson, J., George, J., Wellins, R. and Byman, W. (1994) *Leadership Trapeze: Strategies for Leadership in Team-Based Organizations.* San Francisco: Jossey-Bass.

Index